THE OFFICIAL ILLUSTRATED MOVIE COMPANION

VAMPIRE ACADEMY

BY BRANDON T. SNIDER

razor
bill
RAZORBILL
AN IMPRINT OF PENGUIN GROUP (USA) LLC

RAZORBILL

Published by the Penguin Group
Penguin Group (USA) LLC, 375 Hudson Street, New York, New York 10014, USA

USA | Canada | UK | Ireland | Australia | New Zealand | India | South Africa | China

penguin.com
A Penguin Random House Company

Photographs: Laurie Sparham and Liam Daniel

Library of Congress Cataloging-in-Publication Data is available.

ISBN 978-1-59514-780-6

10 9 8 7 6 5 4 3 2 1

THE OFFICIAL ILLUSTRATED MOVIE COMPANION

VAMPIRE ACADEMY

A massive thank-you goes to the producers, cast, and crew of *Vampire Academy* for taking the time to graciously pass along your wisdom on the process of filmmaking. Your insights were greatly valued and appreciated. Without the following people we wouldn't have a book, and for that we are forever thankful.

Richelle Mead
Mark Waters
Daniel Waters
Deepak Nayar
Michael Preger
Don Murphy
Susan Montford
Lauren Cox
Zoey Deutch
Lucy Fry
Danila Kozlovsky
Sarah Hyland
Dominic Sherwood
Cameron Monaghan
Joely Richardson
Sami Gayle
Olga Kurylenko
Marci Liroff
Reg Poerscout-Edgerton
Frank Walsh
Tony Pierce-Roberts
Ruth Myers
Jimmy O'Dee
John Greaves
Marc Jouveneau
Tom Whitehouse
Roisin Carty
Chris Gill
Charlotte Wright
Jim McCarthy
Russell Binder
Laura Berreitter
Kelli Matthews
Marc Mostman

TABLE OF CONTENTS

Vampire Academy was born out of a couple of simple premises that soon became amazingly complex. While studying Romanian and Russian folktales, I was fascinated by one idea in particular that had a different angle from the "standard" vampire stories we see in American pop culture. It dealt with the concept of two races of vampires—the good Moroi and evil Strigoi—and the half-vampire dhampirs walking between them. Juxtaposed with that was another story I'd been wanting to tell about a bold, in-your-face girl who was unfailingly strong and brave, yet still capable of real emotion and intense loves and friendships. From those elements, Rose Hathaway and the intricate, dangerous world of the Moroi and Strigoi were born. They soon took on a life of their own, becoming far more vivid and detailed than I'd ever dreamed and earning a fan base of millions around the world. The story that began in that first book is still evolving, both in new adventures like the Bloodlines spin-off book series, and in wonderful, artistic graphic-novel and cinema adaptations. This is a world that's alive, vivid, and achingly real, despite its fantastic elements, and I hope you enjoy the ride as much as I do.

— Richelle Mead

CHAPTER 1
BACK TO BASICS

RICHELLE MEAD ON CREATING
Vampire Academy

"I knew when I sat down to write the first Vampire Academy book that I wanted it to be a series. That's how I think when I write. My concepts span books, and I honestly don't know how to write a story that's self-contained in a single volume. Admittedly, that means taking a lot on faith. I knew writing that first book how I wanted Rose's story to end in the last book, but I had no idea if the series would get enough of a following to allow me to write that last book. Nonetheless, I had to go forward and write it and subsequent volumes as though everything would work out as I hoped and planned. I love doing that because when you know your ending, you can seed lots of clues and foreshadowing along the way. That's always more enjoyable to me as a reader, rather than when I get the sense an author pulled out the ending at the last minute in the final book. I was lucky that readers fell in love with the series, allowing me to finish all six volumes and tell the story I'd envisioned."

There's just something about the bright lights of Hollywood that seems to attract young people. Every year, droves of driven adolescents flock to the City of Angels looking for their big break, that one chance to show the world what they're made of. The youthful undead students of St. Vladimir's Academy are no exception, even if they are just characters on the printed page. Drawn from the imagination of author Richelle Mead, *Vampire Academy* is the first in a six-book series that not only became a runaway best seller but also birthed an invigorated fan base and spawned the spin-off series Bloodlines. Now the modern fable is headed for the silver screen, and devotees of Mead's story are bursting with excitement.

The vampire has played a varied role in popular culture and, over time, its admirers have worked overtime to make sure the dark creature's cyclical presence takes up a more permanent space in the lexicon. Thanks in recent years to the popularity of the Twilight series, vampires rose once again as one of the most enduring and fashionable myths around. Though many imitators have hoped to capture the success of past incarnations, many of them have fallen by the wayside due to their sometimes weak and unoriginal content.

Enter: *Vampire Academy.*

Zoey Deutch (Rose Hathaway), Lucy Fry (Lissa Dragomir), and Sarah Hyland (Natalie Dashkov) enjoy a playful moment between scenes.

Richelle Mead's story about the bond between two young women eclipsed expectations and delivered a modern, fresh take on classic vampire mythology. Not one to be done in by overused tropes of the past, Mead drew from previously untouched folklore to craft a story that transcended the genre and propelled the vampire's long and sordid history in a bold new direction. *Vampire Academy* follows the story of best friends Rose Hathaway and Lissa Dragomir as they are pulled back to St. Vladimir's Academy after running away two years before. It was a place they hoped they'd never see again. Theirs is a complicated relationship that takes them both to unexpected places. Lissa is a Moroi princess, a powerful young vampire with mystical abilities who feels cursed by her royal lineage and is struggling to find herself. Rose is Lissa's headstrong guardian protector, a position she may not be quite ready for but one that she feels compelled to fill, regardless. They're brought back to the school by guardian Dimitri Belikov, who becomes Lissa's official bodyguard while Rose is relegated to the sidelines for more training. Now the girls must face the future as they reconcile events from their pasts while dark forces from within the community seek to rip their bond asunder.

Mead's story is thick with vampiric imagery and folklore, but those elements are just part of a larger, more important tale. The backdrop of St. Vladimir's Academy allows Mead's heroines a chance to experience the dramatic ups and downs that come with burgeoning adulthood. Just as any typical teenager deals with gossip, peer pressure, and the pangs of young love, so do Rose and Lissa. Together the two young women take ownership of their lives and the choices they've made, and though they can be sensitive and emotional, make no mistake—they're not to be trifled with. They fight to the death to stand up for what they believe in. Thematically, Mead confronted numerous emotional issues like survivor's guilt and depression, blending fantasy with reality to

create an exciting new world all her own. Mead also didn't forget her readers' obsession with young, forbidden love and made sure to include a variety of male complications for Rose and Lissa. But where did it all start? Where did Richelle Mead come up with this impressive allegory? The answer lies in her desire to give young readers a contemporary narrative that explored the impressive folkloric history of the vampire.

The genesis of Vampire Academy began when Mead was busy working on two different book projects for adult readers: the Succubus series with Georgina Kincaid and the Dark Swan series featuring freelance shaman-for-hire Eugenie Markham. Eying the future, she began to stew on the story possibilities that ancient vampire mythology had not explored previously.

"The idea for Vampire Academy was first conceived back in 2006," Mead explained. "I was already working on two adult series and really wanted to do something for young adults. Since my first two series dealt with demons and fairies respectively, I thought I'd give vampires a try in order to be different— little knowing what a phenomenon they'd become in the next year. I knew from some college courses that a lot of the best vampire mythology could be found in eastern Europe, so I went digging around the stories from that region and eventually discovered Moroi, Strigoi, and dhampirs. Really, all I had to work with was a snippet from that myth, but I was able to build an entire culture and history for my books surrounding those three races and their interactions with each other. The idea of a young woman in love with her instructor was a story I'd wanted to do for some time. Rose's character and personality were, in some ways, inspired by one of my adult characters: Eugenie from the Dark Swan series. Eugenie's another action heroine who's

Olga Kurylenko (Kirova) and Gabriel Byrne (Victor Dashkov) focus on the matter at hand.

Author Richelle Mead with director Mark Waters

not afraid to get in a fight, but she's a twenty-something woman who has already come to terms with who she is and who she wants to be. I began to wonder what it'd be like to write about a younger character, one who was kick-ass and not afraid to stand up for her beliefs, but who was still growing, finding her identity, and also learning what it means to control her fighter impulses. I was fascinated by the idea of that journey. Rose and her fierce devotion to her friends were the results of my experiment, and she soon developed into the unique and vivid character we love today."[1]

Vampire Academy was finally published by Razorbill, an imprint of the Penguin Group, in August 2007 and went on to become a *New York Times* best seller. It produced five follow-up novels: *Frostbite*,

Deepak Nayar prepares to crack a coconut, a tradition in India to celebrate the beginning of an auspicious undertaking.

Shadow Kiss, *Blood Promise*, *Spirit Bound*, and *Last Sacrifice*. While those books continued to follow the story of Rose and Lissa's friendship to its presumed conclusion, Mead wasn't done with St. Vladimir's just yet. In August 2011, readers were treated to an all-new saga featuring ancillary characters from the Vampire Academy books in a series called Bloodlines. After the success of this world, it was inevitable that Hollywood would come knocking. But the road to the silver screen can be a long and arduous trek. When Preger Entertainment first optioned the rights for a *Vampire Academy* film, Mead was cautiously optimistic about the process of bringing her characters to a viewing audience. At the time, she recognized the need to appease her die-hard fans while inviting new ones into the fold.

"It's such a funny thing, the movie business," Mead said back then. "There's no action going on right now. There's no production, no casting, no scripting. There's nothing for me to be involved in at the moment. They're certainly in touch all the time. Right now, they're out soliciting studios and writers. People write to me like, 'Richelle, make sure when you hold auditions . . .' I know my involvement won't be to that extent," she said, laughing. "But Preger Entertainment is a wonderful company. They talk to me a lot. They talk to the fans a lot, which is amazing. They've got this huge Facebook page, where they're

Producer Deepak Nayar joins Richelle Mead for a quick photo during a set visit.

always asking, 'Who would you like to see? What's your favorite part in the book?' I'm sad at the fact that I know there are going to be fans who will never be happy with any adaptation; I feel bad for them. There are people all the time who are like, 'Don't ruin the books!' I've made my peace with the fact—I had to, otherwise I wouldn't have optioned it—that with a movie, it's not going to be the book verbatim. I'm not saying I want a bad adaptation, but I've prepared myself that some things may be different, and that's okay," she reasoned. "I'm kind of Zen with it right now, but that's easy to do when nothing's in production."[2]

As she played the waiting game, Mead was able to solicit the advice of a seasoned pro who'd also seen her characters take on a new life of their own, albeit in the medium of television. Charlaine Harris knew all about the struggle to bring her vision to life, having seen her series of Sookie Stackhouse novels become the runaway

HBO hit series *True Blood*.

"I actually talked to Charlaine Harris a number of times," Mead disclosed. "She's really sweet. She's so down to earth. It was interesting to hear her perspective on that. She's got a real open-minded view to the process of adaptation and how that worked out. It's nice to hear a good success story and to have that on the horizon."[3]

Not long after, the *Vampire Academy* film began to take shape as veteran director Mark Waters was brought on board to direct the adaptation, with his brother Daniel Waters scripting. With Mark having previously directed the teen comedy *Mean Girls* and Daniel having written the cult classic *Heathers*, Mead knew that her characters were in good hands with these two very talented men.

"It's got some *Mean Girls* humor in it. They both have that dark humor going on. It must run in the family. But I wouldn't say it's a comedy. I wouldn't say its irreverent, like 'oh, ha-ha' slapstick.

It's kinda what I said earlier, it goes a lot of different ways. It's got those moments where you do crack up, because somebody, usually Rose, says something so ridiculous. And then something in the next scene, your heart just stops 'cause there is just something emotionally groundbreaking going on. And in the next scene you know it's staking vampires or, you know, whatever. There is some of that, for sure, but I think *Mean Girls* was more comedy in its ratio. I guess. It had its emotional components as well. But for people who like that sense of humor, they are going to like that they will see pieces of that in this. What surprised me about the script was how true it is to the book. As an author, when you sell your options and you turn it over to a screenwriter you never know what is going to happen. I was blown away at just how the script not only follows all the main beats of the book—all the pivotal scenes are there—it really just gets the spirit that I try to convey in my books. My books are always this mix of one part is humorous, and another part you have this deep emotional component, and then there is action running through it. And all of that is there. Daniel Waters just nailed all of that. He got all of that. He understood what I was trying to do. He understands the characters, and I was just kind of amazed. I remember when I finished I looked up at my husband and was like, 'We've got this, babe. Look what they did. It's amazing.'"[4]

"There are these big, high-drama, and romance moments in the Vampire Academy series, for sure," Mead explains. "But there's also a dark, snarky tone as well to offset the melodrama. And those guys are masters at that."[5] But she's also quick to note that *Vampire Academy* "is not a cutesy movie." She explains: "There's this dark humor that runs through it all . . . You're going to laugh at things you probably think you shouldn't laugh at and

The camera operator readies his shot outside the halls of St. Vladimir's Academy.

The crew makes sure the camera is positioned at just the right angle.

you're going to be gripping your seat for the action."[6]

With the creative team in place, everyone's attention turned to the casting process as a fleet of young, hopeful actors crossed their fingers and waited anxiously to see if they'd be among the lucky ones. Soon Zoey Deutch would be announced as the film's Rose Hathaway, Lucy Fry was to become Lissa Dragomir, and Danila Kozlovsky would take on the role of Dimitri Belikov. Rounding out the cast was a slew of up-and-coming actors such as Sarah Hyland as Natalie Dashkov and Cameron Monaghan as Mason Ashford, as well as established and respected names like Gabriel Byrne as Victor Dashkov and Joely Richardson as Queen Tatiana.

"The cast is just spot-on. I am so thrilled with the way that they did this casting," Mead explained at the time. "Everyone was just, I feel, very handpicked. The director was so conscientious about matching the characters' personalities with them. I think the one that most . . . Gosh, it's really hard to pick anyone I would say is the most . . . I mean Zoey [Deutch] has that vibrancy and energy that Rose has. Danila [Kozlovsky]'s got that stoic Dimitri thing going down. Maybe it's because he's a little older than the rest of the cast,

which is exactly how it should be for the books. I think the one that kind of just really knocked me out was when I saw Cameron Monaghan cast as Mason. He is just such a dead ringer for the Mason in my head, which is bittersweet for those who know Mason and the rest of the series. I look and I just think, 'Aw, Cameron.' But yeah, they all are just—I couldn't be more thrilled with the way it panned out. [The script] helped make it real. And I have already sort of commented on how amazed I was. How spot-on it was. So that was one thing. But I think the casting announcements that followed shortly after really just knocked it into the next level. 'Cause, I mean, it happens all the time in Hollywood—people get all excited and they are talking about, 'Yes, yes, we are gonna make this project, it's gonna happen,' and then it just fizzles out. People can talk all they want, but when you reach that point where you are actually getting actors signed on and committed, that is a huge step. Of course it can still fall apart at any point, unfortunately. So when the announcement came out that they had cast Zoey Deutch, Danila Kozlovsky, and Lucy Fry as the three leads, that was big. Those are the three iconic characters and we had faces for them. Not only that, we had the actors who were talking about how excited they were. For me and the fans, that was what actually said, 'Oh my God, this might actually be a movie.'"[7]

And though she didn't have a direct hand in crafting the film itself, Mead happily resigned herself to the process of filmmaking, putting her faith and trust in the assembled professionals to bring her ultimate vision to the screen. "Most of my involvement has just been advisory and a lot of fact-checking. I haven't really spoken to any of the actors outside of social media, but I've talked to Mark and Daniel Waters quite a bit—especially Mark, being the director who has his finger on the pulse of the movie and directing all the details—he's been very thorough about talking to me and checking the details that even surprised me, and I'm delighted that he's doing that because I know that's not a courtesy a lot of authors get. I think a lot of authors are surprised when they walk into a theater to see what became of their movie. But Mark has written me in the past just about like, 'Is this an okay costume choice?' or 'If I do this, is this going to affect something further down in the series?' He's just so thoughtful about everything he does in getting the truest story we can get. So

that's been my role, and I am really happy with that. I like that balance. I don't make movies. A lot of fans expect me to, like, be out there rolling with the camera and doing stuff, and that's not me. You know, I write the books and I am content to do that. I like this balance, you know, that the people who are experts in bringing this visual world to life, you know, they check with me to make sure it's been captured from the book correctly. I think it's a system that has worked out pretty well from everything that I have seen."[8]

With all the key elements locked into place, principal photography began on the *Vampire Academy* film in May 2013. The shoot lasted three months and took the cast and crew from the United States to the United Kingdom. Despite pop culture's romantic notion of filmmaking, the road to making a movie is often a long and arduous journey. What begins as one vision must sometimes evolve and adapt to accommodate the needs of the story. It's a simple fact of the creative process and a crucial part of bringing fiction's best and brightest characters to a wider audience. And in the case of Rose, Lissa, and the rest of the students at St. Vladimir's Academy, they deserve nothing less.

Mark Waters confers with Richelle Mead.

Sarah Hyland, Producer Deepak Nayar, and Danila Kozlovsky

"Filmmaking is such a big canvas, and I love painting on it and telling different stories. There is no other medium like it."

—DEEPAK NAYAR

CHAPTER 2

FACULTY MEETING

DEEPAK NAYAR
Producer Spotlight

Producer Deepak Nayar has built an eclectic résumé since beginning his career in India. As the founder of Kintop Pictures, Nayar produced critically acclaimed films like David Lynch's *Lost Highway* and Wim Wenders's *Buena Vista Social Club*, in addition to popular favorites such as *Bend It Like Beckham* and *Dredd*. His films have also appeared around the world in prestigious film festivals while earning Oscar, Golden Globe, and BAFTA nominations along the way.

"I've been a producer for over twenty years," Nayar explained. "I initially started working as a production assistant on films in India. Then I moved to the United States and started working as David Lynch's driver on the pilot of *Twin Peaks*. I worked my way up through the ranks, eventually becoming Lynch's producer on *Lost Highway*. It ended up being an important journey, teaching me everything that I needed to know about filmmaking." During that time, Nayar learned every aspect of the entertainment business, eventually settling on one of the most important roles in the filmmaking process. "As a producer, other producers come to me when they're looking to make their projects a reality. Once I commit to a project, I secure the financing and distribution. When that's in place, I ensure that the project is finished and delivered to the level committed to the distributors. The process involves finalizing the shooting script, getting the right cast in place, crew members, locations, and managing the budget. I also make sure the distributors follow through with their commitment of a proper release of the film. You could say I'm involved in every aspect of the filmmaking process while exercising control of business and financial matters." When pressed to name favorites, Nayar finds himself unable to pick just one. "I am fond of all my work; otherwise, given what I do, I could not justify spending the time doing it. Every film takes nearly a

Deepak Nayar with Line Producer Paul Sarony

year out of your life; therefore, I only get involved with projects I like. I love making movies—taking an idea and seeing it all the way to the screen. I love telling stories that touch people's hearts, like *Bend It Like Beckham*. I love movies that are for bringing about change. My film *Bhopal Express* asked questions about the Indian parliament's dealings with foreign corporations. I made a documentary, *Buena Vista Social Club*, to preserve a dying music in Cuba. Filmmaking is such a big canvas, and I love painting on it and telling different stories. There is no other medium like it."

With such an impressive stable of cinema behind him, Nayar brings his keen eye to the film adaptation of *Vampire Academy*. He found the idea of "telling a high-school story set in a different world" to be rich with possibility, and that the

"drama of friendship, love, and intrigue" eschewed typical teenage romance. Thankfully, a partnership was made with Reliance Entertainment, an India-based motion picture company, which allowed Nayar a chance to bring this story to the cinema.

"Reliance Entertainment got involved in *Vampire Academy* under its partnership with Kintop Pictures," Nayar explained. "Anil Ambani and Amitabh Jhunjhunwala supported the project from the onset after optioning the underlying rights to the entire series of Vampire Academy books. They fast-tracked the making of a *Vampire Academy* film by committing to fund the entire budget of the movie. From the time the script was submitted in December 2012 to the film going into preproduction in March 2013, it was only four months. For a picture to be green-lit and shot in such a short period of time is something of an anomaly in the movie business. With such a strong backing from Reliance, it gave the filmmakers the freedom to make the best movie possible, including making choices on cast and crew which were best for the film."

The young cast greatly impressed Nayar and he found that, despite their youth, they excelled at portraying the emotional dynamics in the script with dedication and commitment. "Each of the actors performed their roles incredibly well, and it was very surprising to see how they suited their parts. Since this was independently financed by Reliance Entertainment, we had the flexibility to cast who we thought were perfect for the role—so the whole cast was a case of perfection. All the characters are interesting in some way or another, and each of them contribute to make the experience of watching the film as a whole."

With so many great moments in the film, Nayar found it difficult to choose among his favorites. "It's hard to say there is one favorite; there are so many that I like. Rose getting her ass kicked by Dimitri when they first meet. The Strigoi attack. Meeting Kirova. Rose becoming a strong person. And seeing Lissa perform magic." But it wasn't just the script that excited Nayar; it was the opportunity to bring so many seasoned professionals on board to work their magic. "Frank Walsh did a great job designing the sets, Tony Pierce-Roberts lighting them, and Ruth [Myers] designing the costumes." Never work with children or animals, as the old Hollywood saying goes, but in the case of *Vampire Academy*, Nayar explained that at least one animal in particular, and an unexpected one at

that, was a pleasure to work with. "The psi-hounds were to be a certain breed of trained dogs, but that did not work out for us, so we ended up creating them in CGI," he confessed. "The crow, however, was wonderful. It hit its marks and performed all its tasks with flair."

Though the Vampire Academy fan base is strong, Nayar was keen to bring new and exciting elements to the mythology in order to keep things fresh. "It is always tricky to satisfy fans of books that have a huge following," he explained. "That said, the fans are also looking for a cinematic experience as well, not just a literal translation. It is a fine balance that we try to maintain. Keeping your fan base satisfied is important—but it is also important to tell a good story with universal appeal. The movie has to stand by itself. When we look at making a movie we do not look at what is being cut or not; it is more what works for the film and how best to tell a cinematic story. It's all about creating a journey the audience will like."

Deepak Nayar with Director Mark Waters

Michael Preger and Danila Kozlovsky

IN HIS OWN WORDS: MICHAEL PREGER

Producer

"As primarily a 'development' producer, my role begins by first envisioning a project. This involves a lot of book reading, exploring different ideas, stories, original screenplays, and other original source materials, to find a project that is great dramatically but also something that deserves an adaptation. This is the challenging aspect, to understand what works and what doesn't. There are many fine stories and ideas floating around, but finding something ideally suited for an adaptation is trickier! In *Vampire Academy,* my job was first finding the project, then securing the underlying rights for adaptation of the work, then finding the right team of filmmakers to create it. My career has spanned many sides of the entertainment industry. I started in public TV, and then moved to advertising, then music marketing and distribution business, music videos, TV pilots, indie films, and finally feature films and miniseries.

"*Vampire Academy* is a great story, first and foremost! To further break it down, the relationships between the characters are engaging, interesting, and relatable. The setting and world are fascinating but most of all, for me, it was the strong female relationship between Rose and

Lissa that captured my interest; their independence, self-reliance, and loyalty to one another, above all others. They are the kind of role models that instill a different perception of females in today's world. Something often lacking in today's storytelling. But it doesn't end there. The mythic underpinnings of this vampiric universe are unique. It's not the same old monster story. It's a wonderful setting to explore interesting personality dynamics between the characters. What Richelle has created is a world that challenges the typical clichéd notions of the vampire love triangles of yesteryear. In *Vampire Academy*, she provides a new theme upon which to build a more interesting and complex story that is layered with moments of self-achievement, humor, sarcasm, danger, fear, romance, and terror. Essentially, everything we all deal with throughout our lives and in our relationships. The fans will be the first to tell you this is not just a story of vampires and teenagers. It's more about life itself. Not much had to be cut from the book. It was more about trying to squeeze all the subtleties of the story onto the screen. Creative license was utilized in a few scenes that are original to the film, but this was more for dramatic interpretation. What makes Richelle's story so interesting are the characters who populate it. All of them are there for a reason. They reflect the different types of personalities you often encounter in everyday life. Issues of loyalty, betrayal, greed, revenge, hope, faith, passion, love, loss, tragedy, horror, depression, anxiety . . . It may be fiction but there's something very real within the layers of this story that all audiences, young and old, male or female, connect with. As the screenplay was being developed, the team reached out to Richelle

on numerous occasions. I referred to her as our 'GPS.' Every time we potentially backed ourselves into a corner creatively, we would send Richelle an urgent e-mail titled 'GPS question.' This was done to make every effort to stay within the four walls of her story. The extraordinary thing about this project is that while this is arguably Rose's story, the ensemble of characters is the real strength, like the book series. Casting took place both in the US and the UK. A lot of hard work went into this selection process. The results of this can be seen on the screen. I would venture to say there is a fan base for all of the principal characters in this series— that's one of the more compelling aspects of it. Some characters have been reserved for future installments; a couple have been introduced to round out the events within this adaptation. But the heart of the story comes through and the intrigue is all there. I can't recall another project ever that has had the support and energy of its fans behind it from day one. This project is as much about the social-media presence and dedication of its fans to get this film made as anything else. It has influenced everyone involved in making this picture."

Richelle Mead chatting with Sami Gayle during her visit to the set.

DON MURPHY & SUSAN MONTFORD:
Power Couple

As Hollywood alliances go, you won't find a bond stronger than Don Murphy and Susan Montford's. Together they've produced films such as *Shoot 'Em Up*, *Real Steel,* and *Splice*. Their need for artistic expression began well before they became a married couple. Montford got her start as a director and screenwriter in her native Scotland, where she attended the Glasgow School of Art. After making a handful of short films, one of which screened at the Toronto International Film Festival, she made her way to the United States, where she transitioned to producing. Murphy, on the other hand, graduated with a bachelor of science in business administration from Georgetown University before beginning his career in the entertainment field. After writing movie reviews for his school newspaper and working on advertising campaigns for films at his father's advertising agency, he got a taste for something bigger and enrolled in the USC School of Cinematic Arts in Los Angeles. Murphy eventually found his way to Montford, and the couple produced *While She Was Out*, a thriller starring Kim Basinger that Montford also wrote and directed. After a slew of creative challenges and successes, the couple has teamed up once more to bring their vision and discerning eye to the adaptation of *Vampire Academy*.

Q&A WITH PRODUCER SUSAN MONTFORD

Q: How would you describe your role as a producer?

Don and I work on choosing a writer, developing a script, choosing a director, working with a director on casting, and getting a great crew. Hands-on through the whole process. We both always wanted to be in the film business, me in the UK and Don in America. We met at the Toronto Film Festival and have worked together extensively ever since. We're proud of all our films and we think of them as our children. Most recently we did the Hugh Jackman film *Real Steel* together, and we're very proud of that. Watching a script come to life in three dimensions is the most exciting thing in the world.

Q: What was it about *Vampire Academy* that made it perfect for adapting into a film?

While reading the first three novels, I was struck by the powerful characters and the mythic quality of the books. The third one has all the elements of *The Empire Strikes Back*. I really wanted to see these girls develop on-screen. I wanted to see them challenged by their power of the spirit and their physical prowess.

Dimitri keeps a watchful eye on Rose and Lissa.

school where the students face all the same issues, but in the vampire world.

Q: Which character relationships did you connect to? Were there any characters or situations from the book that changed for story purposes?

Rose and Lissa's dynamic is very relatable and forms the central thread through the story. Kirova's character was also expanded. We had to carefully and considerately streamline and simplify the plot to make it compellingly cinematic.

Q: There's been a lot of positive buzz, and *Vampire Academy* fans are beyond excited for the film. Is it stressful waiting to hear their reaction?

Of course you want the fans to love the cinematic version of what they have been reading. But reading a book allows you to personally and uniquely create the world, whereas watching a movie makes the world concrete; and it's a different experience, hopefully one that heightens the experience of the books and delights the fans.

Q: How would you describe the story in the simplest terms?

After a car accident, two school friends develop a psychic bond, but the school they attend just happens to be "Vampire Academy," where vampires are taught how to live among humans.

Q: Which aspects of the book were you anxious to examine in the film?

I wanted to explore the friendship and bond between two teenage girls, and the responsibility and cost of developing and honoring their talents and gifts. The fact is that "Vampire Academy," the school, is structured like a version of a real high

> "I was struck by the powerful characters and the mythic quality of the books."
>
> — SUSAN MONTFORD

"I really connected to the Vampire Academy book series, and by the end of the third one I felt like it had to be a film. The Lissa/Rose bond, the use of special magic, and the different levels of the vampire society were all unique elements to explore. Richelle's vision was what we all signed up for and adhered to. We've worked closely with the fans, and the excitement in this project comes from, with success, the opportunity to make more."

— DON MURPHY

Q: Do you have any favorite moments from the film?

That one's a spoiler alert—you'll have to wait and see the movie, and then I'm sure you'll know what I'm alluding to.

Q: Did anything surprise you during filming?

No. Except for our continued joy at the great locations and sets.

Q: How important was it to receive Richelle Mead's ultimate blessing when the film first began?

Richelle's involvement was instrumental and she seems to be happy with what she's seen, so far.

Q: The film's cast has built up quite the fan base already. Are there any performances you're anxious to see on-screen?

All the actors were a delight to watch, but Olga Kurylenko and Sami Gayle brought some really interesting twists to their performances.

Q: Any final words to excite people about *Vampire Academy*?

I can't wait for audiences to see just how different this movie is from all the other ones you've seen about vampires. It's irreverent, sexy—and yet deep.

A group of catty students react suspiciously to Rose and Lissa as they arrive at the dance.

"What's funny is that I decided early on that my kick-ass heroine would be a dhampir, simply because I liked the mix of human and vampire traits."

—RICHELLE MEAD

CHAPTER 3
PREP SCHOOL

RICHELLE MEAD ON THE MYTHOLOGY OF *Vampire Academy*

"I took a class at the University of Michigan on Slavic folklore and mythology. One of the units we studied was on vampires, and we had the opportunity to read some really great stories and examine a lot of the symbolism behind those old tales. Years later, when I decided to write a vampire novel, I decided I wanted to base my series out of that same region. So I went searching through eastern European mythology again and eventually found a reference to Moroi and Strigoi that I thought could really make a great foundation for a vampire society. Dhampirs are a little widespread in pop culture, and I'd heard of them before, though they, too, come from this same region. What's funny is that I decided early on that my kick-ass heroine would be a dhampir, simply because I liked the mix of human and vampire traits. Later, I learned that in a lot of eastern European myths, dhampirs have a reputation for being great vampire hunters. There were those who believed that if an evil vampire was causing trouble, you needed to recruit a dhampir to come get rid of him or her. So, without even realizing it, I'd cast Rose in a traditional warrior role!"[9]

Zoey Deutch as the feisty Rose Hathaway

Rose Hathaway and Dimitri Belikov train for battle.

DHAMPIR

Dhampirs are willing humans who have offered themselves as a source of nourishment to a Moroi in exchange for protection against evil forces. Nourishment comes in the form of blood, which is ritualistically drained from a dhampir's body as needed. There is an unexplainable and unique bond between the dhampirs and Moroi that transcends the seemingly simplistic nature of their relationship. Dhampirs often feel a great rush of endorphins when a Moroi uses them to feed. This surge is caused by the chemicals in vampire saliva, and if dhampirs aren't careful, they can find themselves painfully addicted to the mystical experience. A *blood whore* is a crude and derogatory term used to describe a dhampir who allows a Moroi vampire to drink her blood during sex, a practice that is frowned upon by the vampire society. A dhampir is typically born of a Moroi-human relationship and can only safely reproduce with Moroi. Physically they're of a thicker, more human build than the other vampire factions. This stockier frame helps them guard the Moroi against Strigoi attacks. Though the Moroi do drink blood, they also consume normal food for sustenance. If Moroi are without a steady supply of fresh blood, they will weaken after only two short days. If a source of energy isn't found, they will grow increasingly frail and eventually perish.

И - БОЙ

И1 И2 И3
И4 И5 И6
И7 И8 И9
И10 И11 И12

Ф - РАЗМИНКА

Ф1 Ф2 Ф3
Ф4 Ф5 Ф6
Ф7 Ф8 Ф9
Ф10 Ф11 Ф12

GUARDIAN

Dhampirs who have dedicated their lives to serve and protect a Moroi are known as guardians. Because dhampirs are born of both a human and a Moroi, their survival depends on the survival of the Moroi bloodline. The role of the guardian has historically been of great importance as the Strigoi have attempted, over the centuries, to wreak havoc on their Moroi enemies. There's a rigorous and time-consuming amount of training that guardians must endure in order to serve. They're educated in a multitude of enhanced fighting styles and are required to undergo countless tests over a period of time to ensure that they're fully prepared to commit themselves to servitude for life. Generally it is the male dhampirs who take on the challenge of guardianship while the females choose to remain domestic. Most Moroi are given a guardian at a designated age, and those Moroi who are of a royal bloodline are given preferential treatment. When guardians have successfully completed their training, they receive a promise mark signifying that they have graduated to the next level and are ready to protect their Moroi ward full-time against the Strigoi.

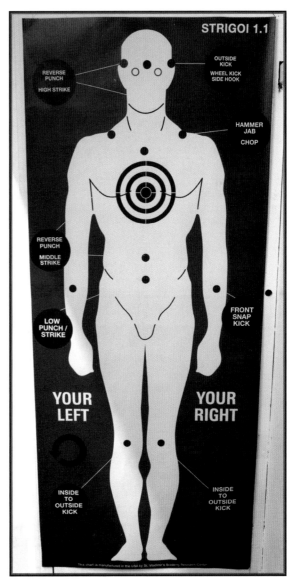

STRIGOI 1.1

REVERSE PUNCH
HIGH STRIKE

OUTSIDE KICK
WHEEL KICK SIDE HOOK

HAMMER JAB
CHOP

REVERSE PUNCH
MIDDLE STRIKE

LOW PUNCH / STRIKE

FRONT SNAP KICK

YOUR LEFT

YOUR RIGHT

INSIDE TO OUTSIDE KICK

INSIDE TO OUTSIDE KICK

Ashley Charles enjoys a little snack as the Moroi royal Jesse Zeklos.

Queen Tatiana, the regal leader of the Moroi, as played by Joely Richardson.

MOROI

The Moroi vampire is at peace with his or her place in the social strata, as opposed to the cold and malicious Strigoi. They're blessed with a kindness and compassion that comes from the fact that they are indeed born mortal, a "living vampire," as they are typically known. Physically they form an enchanting silhouette, tall and slim compared to their counterparts. The females are often said to be endowed with an almost supernatural beauty. Though they shun the sunlight, Moroi are not opposed to being outside during daytime hours as long as they find a delicate balance. The Moroi possess the ability to perform elemental magic by harnessing the power of water, air, fire, earth, or spirit. For a period of time, the spirit element was forgotten and dismissed, and Moroi who specialized in mastering that particular magic were seen as having no specialty at all. Moroi are also possessed of an ability called compulsion. By making eye contact with their mark, they can take control of that person's will, allowing them to control their every thought and movement. Moroi are forbidden to use elemental powers offensively; they can be used only in self-defense or the defense of others. Though most of them understand that rule, it can often cause anger and frustration for Moroi when they feel threatened. It's for this reason they are placed with guardians, whose sole purpose is to protect the Moroi from harm and help guide them on an honorable path.

RICHELLE MEAD ON
Moroi Powers

"People often ask, 'If the Moroi don't use magic for fighting, what do they use it for?' The answer is that in recent history, most Moroi have simply used their powers for ordinary, day-to-day tasks. That might seem like a waste to some people, but if I had a chance to use air magic, I would do it in an instant! I absolutely hate blow-drying my hair and would love to zap it into place each morning."[10]

Strigoi vampires come in all shapes and sizes.

STRIGOI

While the Moroi and dhampirs have found a delicate and peaceful balance in their association, the immortal Strigoi dream only of terror and destruction. A Strigoi vampire is undead, having been made and not born. A Moroi vampire can be turned Strigoi by drinking the blood of another Strigoi, by force or voluntarily. But Moroi vampires can also *choose* to become Strigoi by killing the person they're feeding on. This is considered one of the most heinous acts that can be committed by a Moroi. After turning, a Strigoi is consumed with the blinding bloodlust, squarely focused on their former Moroi brethren. Though they often feast on whatever they can get their hands on, they crave the magical blood of the Moroi like no other. Because of its supernatural properties, it gives them enhanced strength and agility, making them difficult to destroy. Visually, they can be terrifying creatures with their milky-white complexion and blazing-red pupils, but when confronted with sunlight their skin will burst into flames, causing them intense agony. Strigoi have no moral code and are forbidden to walk upon holy ground. There are only two ways to kill a Strigoi. The first is a simple decapitation. The second is through the use of a special silver stake. This unique weapon must be forged with each of the elements and then stabbed directly through a Strigoi's heart. This act will kill a Strigoi instantly, but if the stake is enchanted with healing magic, the Strigoi will revert to his or her former Moroi form.

Novice Moroi have control over the spectrum of elements, but as they grow older, they are encouraged to embrace only one of these special magical abilities in order to focus their powers.

AIR

An air user can manipulate a gentle breeze into an enormous gust of wind, a handy tactic used to knock a combatant to the ground. Or, if they're without any recourse, air users can draw the breath from Strigoi enemies, leaving them to suffocate.

EARTH

An earth user has total control over terra firma and can use the planet's crust to their advantage. This means they can use mud, rock, and wood to hurl at their enemies, or they can focus their energy into creating massive and destructive earthquakes.

WATER

Water users can manipulate any form of water and turn it into a deadly weapon by drawing it into their enemy's body to drown them. Water can also be wielded in a much less violent way, as a low-level distraction or diversion.

FIRE

The fire element is one of the most dynamic elements, but also one of the most brutal. Fire users have incredible range. They might simply warm the air around enemies in order to stifle them, or they could violently set them ablaze if need be.

SPIRIT

Instead of pulling from the natural elements, spirit users get their abilities from their own powerful essence. Their strength comes from within, which makes the use of such powers incredibly taxing. Using too much spirit magic can induce mood swings and depression and, in extreme cases, even drive a Moroi completely mad. A spirit user is able to enchant certain objects for use in self-defense, one example being the silver stake used to destroy Strigoi. They're also able to heal both plants and animals and, when needed, bring a recently deceased person back to life. This act leaves the newly reborn person one of the "shadow kissed" who is then psychically bound to the spirit user.

COMPULSION

Spirit magic users have the arcane capacity for compulsion, though the abuse of such magic is forbidden. Compulsion allows the user to forcibly manipulate the thoughts or feelings of others, making them do and say things against their wills.

GUARDIAN *Marks*

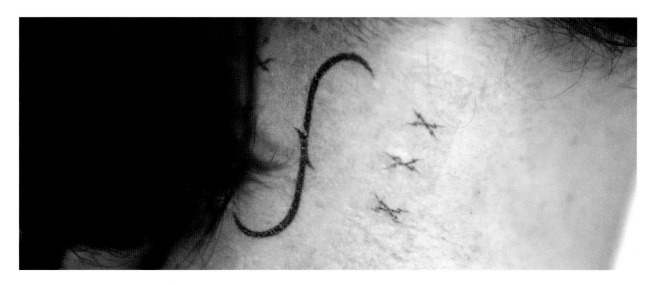

RICHELLE MEAD ON *Guardian Tattoos*

"The guardian tattoos came about for a couple of different reasons. One was that I wanted a way to establish rank and honor among the guardians. I wanted people to know at a glance who the most powerful dhampirs are. It was also important to me to establish a unique culture for the dhampirs. So much of what they do is in service to the Moroi that it's easy to forget the dhampirs are their own people. The tattoo system and its ceremonies give the guardians an opportunity to have something that is totally their own. What I most certainly did not expect was that readers would start getting those same guardian tattoos permanently applied in real life! I've seen some pretty amazing tattoo work at my signings that I never envisioned when I started the series. I just hope my readers are still glad they got those tattoos twenty years from now!"[11]

PROMISE MARK

When dhampirs complete their training and graduate to guardianship, they receive an ornate promise-mark tattoo on the base of their necks that resembles a twisting snake. This mark signifies the dhampirs' promise to protect their Moroi wards at all costs, even if it means sacrificing their own lives.

MOLNIJA

When guardians have done their duty and killed attacking Strigoi, they are awarded a *molnija* mark to signify their bravery in the face of danger. *Molnija* is Russian for *lightning*, and the crest itself looks like two lightning bolts crossing one another.

ZVEZDA

When guardians have successfully destroyed hordes of Strigoi, they are branded with the battle mark known as zvezda. This designation is the mark of a true fighter and is shaped like a star, which is what the word *zvezda* means in Russian.

ALCHEMIST *Tattoos*

In the Middle Ages, there were groups of crafty tinkerers who believed they could alter the properties of lead, magically turning it into precious gold. While they were never actually able to make this happen, they did follow their mystic inclinations, leading them farther down a path to the occult. Eventually they discovered the world of vampires and began working with the Moroi to hide their presence from the mortal world. Alchemists were bestowed a tattoo made of gold and Moroi blood, which gave them abilities similar to those of the Moroi themselves, such as prolonged life and enduring health. Each tattoo is magically charmed with water and earth compulsion magic that prevents the alchemist from revealing any information about the Moroi's existence.

Screenwriter Daniel Waters takes a moment to ponder on the set of *Vampire Academy.*

"Not only do Dan Waters and I have the same birth day (maybe not the same year), but we're basically best friends forever. I so appreciate the world and words he's created. I hope I've done justice to one or two of his jokes. PS, I heart Dan."

—ZOEY DEUTCH ON SCREENWRITER DANIEL WATERS

CHAPTER 4
APPLICATION PROCESS

Q&A WITH *VAMPIRE ACADEMY* SCREENWRITER DANIEL WATERS

The art of the adaptation is a tricky thing. While the public loves to see its favorite literary heroes on the silver screen, the unique ability to capture the magic of the page and translate it into film can be wrought with complications. What works in print doesn't always work in visual media. How does one writer maintain another writer's original vision while adding something fresh to the overall concept? A capable writer could play it safe and cater solely to the wants and needs of the audience, but where's the fun in that? A writer wants to bring their own voice to the material and give it a kick in the pants. Of course it took more than just a *capable* writer to bring the characters of St. Vladimir's to the screen—it took an *exceptional* one.

Natalie, Lissa, and Rose make a startling discovery.

Daniel Waters has built a unique and diverse résumé over the years, famously penning pop favorites like *Batman Returns* and *Demolition Man*. But it was a black comedy about a group of social-climbing high school girls called *Heathers* that would ultimately be his most memorable. As luck would have it, Waters's deft handling of those characters made him the perfect person to bring Richelle Mead's world to the big screen. And it didn't hurt that his brother Mark was the director, either.

Q: Your brother Mark directed the film, but this is the first time you've actually worked together in this capacity. What was that experience like at this stage in your careers? Is there a language that you have with each other that made it easier for you to communicate creatively?

This is the first film that's been made, but we've developed a lot of things because we always knew we'd make a great team . . . kind of like Dustin Hoffman and Tom Cruise in *Rain Man*! I've always been the crazy, occasionally handicapped, occasionally amazing older brother, and he's always been the type A, hotshot younger brother who gets things done. I'm the imaginative right brain and he's the analytical left brain. It's been said that the ultimate desired alchemy in making a movie

is that your writer be brilliant and your director be smart. As my brother's wife puts it, "Danny makes Mark cool, Mark makes Danny coherent."

Our sensibilities are pretty similar (*Heathers* is to *Mean Girls* what Joy Division is to New Order) and, outside of my hate and his love for *Love Actually*, we pretty much assess every movie we see the same way. That said, as a writer and as a director, I've always had the problem that I never met a tone I didn't like. My brother sets out a vision on the horizon of what the final movie should be and never wavers, while I'm like a cat reacting to a laser pointer. When you have as many varied elements as *Vampire Academy* does—supernatural thriller, romance, and comedy—keeping intact a specific tone and vision is of paramount importance. The cast, the crew, and I were quite happy that Mark was the gatekeeper . . . even if that meant doing things over and over to get exactly what he wanted.

Q: How did you end up adapting *Vampire Academy* for the screen? Was this a job that you sought or were you asked to write it based on previous experience?

Before the clouds parted and the golden rays of Richelle Mead's novel shined down upon me, I had never heard of it. I was in my own little world of making R-rated films that only twelve people were seeing when big-producer pals of mine, Don Murphy and Susan Montford, contacted me. Treating me like a samurai master who hasn't pulled his sword in many years, they asked me to return to the realm of high school—but a high school like no other.

There's no getting around that hearing the words *Vampire Academy* without reading the book does not inspire a lot of excitement from an adult male. *Has it come to this? I'm being offered a Saturday morning cartoon where I have to come up with lines like, "Call a dentist, I've got a fang-ache!"* I trusted Don and Susan, so I dived in . . . and quickly knew that this was material I could respond to.

As much as I enjoyed the novel, all the Vampire Academy novels, I couldn't avoid the fact that a definite fatigue had set in certain places, namely planet Earth, over the whole vampire genre: "Do we really need another vampire movie?" I then reminded myself that when people are tired of a genre, that's when you can get a little crazy, a little wicked, a little subversive; lull people in with what they think they know about a genre and then *smack* them.

It's the same approach I took with my screenplay *Heathers*, which came at time when people were exhausted by the teen film genre. I should put on my card: "Tired of a genre? Call Daniel Waters." Nothing makes me more happy than being able to wipe the smug smirk off someone who says, "Oh, I know exactly what this movie is going to be like . . ." Of course, this is an adaptation and it sure helps when the novel you are adapting is chock-full of humor, romance, adventure, and blood whores.

Q: What themes did you connect to from the book series? As the man who gave us the film *Heathers*, what is it about young women in a dark setting that interests you?

As my ex-girlfriends can attest to, it's not like I'm some dazzling feminist, but I've always strived for originality in what I write and what I read. I find that stories with male protagonists have been done to death throughout history . . . and hey, we're not that complex. Female protagonists, when they have more on their minds than finding Mr. Right, are inherently fascinating because the world has put women in a zone that makes the world feel comfortable. When a woman breaks out of her assigned role, the effect is always unpredictable and entertaining.

We all hear of the solemn need for "strong female characters," but even limiting them to "strong" seems lame. Winona Ryder's character, Veronica Sawyer, in *Heathers*; my take on Selina Kyle/Catwoman in *Batman Returns*; and now (on

Daniel and Mark Waters enjoy a brotherly moment between scenes.

loan from Richelle Mead) Rose Hathaway, are more than strong. Sometimes they are weak . . . sometimes hilarious . . . violent . . . vulgar . . . enigmatic . . . I say pile on those adjectives!

On a very basic level, the world needs more female protagonists. I'm kind of perturbed that people feel the need to compare Rose Hathaway and Bella Swan from *Twilight*. Why do we keep feeling the need to pit female characters against each other? Nobody says, "Wow, Iron Man sure has a better sense of humor than Wolverine." Uh, yeah, they're completely different characters.

Q: In one sentence, give us the distilled premise of the film *Vampire Academy*.

Answering that question is more difficult than actually writing the script! The fact that *Vampire Academy* is not a describe-in-one-sentence kind of book is what first appealed to me, but here it goes:

After running away, two best friends are dragged back to their unique boarding school to face the everyday problems of homework, boys, parties, vampire feeding schedules, psychic bonds, the pressure of declaring a magic, terrifying threats, and most troubling of all, the repressed

memories of why they left the Academy in the first place.

You didn't say it couldn't be a run-on sentence!

Q: What were some elements from the *Vampire Academy* world that you felt stood out as unique and important to expound upon?

It seems like the first half hour of every movie now has some wide-eyed innocent discovering a secret world and having to be brought up to speed with a lot of squeals of "This is impossible . . . This can't be happening!" What a relief that we hit the ground running in *Vampire Academy*, only dealing with characters already familiar with the world, allowing the viewer alone to be the innocent. It's like getting to go backstage at a concert rather than sitting outside in the fortieth row. As a moviegoing society, we are past the point of characters saying, "Oh my gosh, you're a vampire! But there's no such thing as vampires!"

My brother's and my single most important mission in adapting *Vampire Academy* was managing the alchemy between action-packed, mystery-laden vampire film, and humorous, laid-back teen film. If you have been a vampire all your

Rose protects her best friend.

life, you are not going to shout, "Oh no, my fangs are coming out, must suck blood." You will casually walk over to the feeder clinic the way someone would go to the cafeteria.

It was important to my brother and me, no matter how insane things get to the viewer, that the characters stay natural and grounded in the real world of high school. Vampires can be bullies, vampires can be lonely, vampires can feel the pain of first love, vampires can fail their magic classes if they don't study . . . and then when we get everybody relaxed, thinking they are just watching a fun high school movie with fangs . . . *that's* when we pull out the Strigoi.

Q: In translating a book for the screen, were there any aspects that were hard to manage or reconcile? Any elements that had to be cut or diminished?

When I read the book for the first time, I loved it. When I read the book again thinking purely in terms of making it into a movie, there was still good lovin', but like the girlfriend who suddenly becomes your wife, I became angry and frustrated by a couple things. Some of the best works of literature have unreliable narrators, but I found Rose to be

annoyingly selective in the information she was holding back from us—I guess that's why teenage girls relate to her so well!

I threw the book across the room when Rose happens to reveal that [paraphrasing], "Oh, yeah, did I forget to mention Ms. Karp turned herself into a Strigoi?" Uh, *what*?!? I can understand why Rose may want to keep that 411 from delicate Lissa, but not the reader! When I picked the book back up from the ground, I realized I had come upon the key to making the novel into a movie . . . It was my turn to keep information from Rose!

You see, I was having a problem that the girls, in many ways, sit around waiting for new information and new dead animals to drop in their laps (a novel can get away with that more than a movie, especially when we are caught up in Richelle's writing), but making the fate of Ms. Karp and even the true nature of why Rose and Lissa left the Academy in the first place into actual mysteries that the girls must proactively investigate—it suddenly gave the film an engine.

The elements of the movie are still mostly from Rose's point of view, but she is no longer in control of all the facts, which makes things a lot more cinematic. At its bare bones, the adaptation process was taking the story out of Rose's head and putting it on-screen.

Q: Is it difficult for you to cut stuff? When adapting something, does it make it easier to leave things behind?

Ask any writer and they will tell you it is easier to kill somebody else's children than your own children, but I tried to be a compassionate murderer. Richelle and her more sane fans realize that to demand that the experience of reading the book be exactly like the experience of watching the film diminishes both experiences. Even if I did give Richelle's less sane fans their five-hour movie depicting every single moment in the book, it wouldn't have the same effect and even they would fall asleep.

I cannot attempt to replace the singular and intimate relationship one has with the book. I thought of the whole process as having to put a bowl of all this amazing, magical gunpowder into a single bullet for maximum impact . . . I'm going to pack as much as I can into the bullet, but it's not all going to get in there. The cinematic steel casing to harness the gunpowder in is something I have to create myself . . . which means new transitions, new consolidations, and some entirely new beats. Now, the fan who wails that I cut Eddie Castile from the movie, even though he's got like three lines in the first book, will notice what's missing, but a film simply has different structural demands than a novel. I kept everyone's favorite scenes intact, but not necessarily in the order they read them.

If you were to make a graph of Rose and Lissa's friendship in the book, there would be a lot of jagged, up-and-down lines: They love each other and then they are mad at each other, instantly going from shopping trips to silent treatments . . . For a film, unlike a book or a TV series or even real life, the graph has to be a lot smoother: basically one clean stroke up, one clean stroke down, one clean stroke up again. We established a clear narrative of dhampir runs away with Moroi, dhampir loses Moroi (à la Lissa's mental unraveling during Operation Brainwash), dhampir gets Moroi back. Definitely great little details are lost in the process of this restructuring, but that's what the book is for. We want

Deepak Nayar, Daniel Waters, and Mark Waters

the viewers who have never read the book to rush out and get it after the movie is over!

Q: Which character or dynamic did you find the most interesting to write? Did any characters disappoint you?

Do you really need to ask what dynamic I found the most interesting to write? The bond between complete opposites/best friends Rose Hathaway and Lissa Dragomir is *the* great dynamic in the history of young-adult literature. On the simplest level—take away the fangs, the blood, and the guardian oaths—you have one girl who can never hide anything from her best friend and another girl who knows more about her bestie than anyone would ever want to know . . . It's such a delicious, fertile take on female friendship that I could write about it forever without even bothering to bring in Strigoi, psi-hounds, or feeders.

The one character I had a lot of trouble with was Mia . . . she is *so* brash and over-the-top that I thought she would come across as a cartoon on-screen. I like my cinematic bitches a little less in-your-face. I tried to make Mia somewhat more sly, and gave her actual game as someone capable of being an actual villain.

I'm not sure how successful I was, but thankfully Sami Gayle, the actress playing Mia, crushed it. She was in literally one of the first shots of the very first day of filming and brought more emotion and complexity to the part than I ever thought possible. Even Sami's short hair I thought to be a helpful de-cartooning of book-Mia's "Cabbage Patch" ringlets. I actually felt bad when she got punched . . . I mean, is the punishment for slut-shaming more slut-shaming? It made the Rose-Mia dynamic much more layered.

One of the first things I asked Richelle Mead when I met her was, "So who's the real Mia? Someone from your high school that you want to get back at?!"

Q: What's your favorite piece of dialogue in the script?

My favorite piece of dialogue is when Lissa says to Rose: "Boys are weak and sweaty piglets, beneath our concern. That is our covenant."

Q: Did you have to combine any characters from the rest of the series in order to tell a more effective story?

I know how much fans just *love* when adapters do that to their favorite novels . . . so I tried to avoid it. Certainly I read all the books in the series before adapting the first one, so there were definitely stray bits and character quirks that I brought up into the first film. Face it, if the world doesn't embrace the first film, the others ain't happening . . . I let Rose handle a silver stake one book earlier (Sorry, Dimitri!). Also, I am of the belief that a girl cannot keep a secret from her best friend that involves having an illicit crush for more than twenty-four hours, so Rose definitely lets Lissa in on certain personal-life aspects sooner.

The girls have a catchphrase that they aptly use throughout the first film: "For us, weird doesn't begin to cover it." I thought

I had brilliantly invented it, but I realized it's from *Frostbite* . . . so who knows what else I did subconsciously.

Q: What did you feel you added to the Vampire Academy mythos?

Uh-oh, you start throwing the word *mythos* around and I get scared. I would not dare touch Richelle's mythos! Yes, I've refurbished the structure of the first *Vampire Academy*, tried to make the characters a little sharper and wittier, increased the action, raised the stakes (pardon the pun), but all in service of maintaining the *soul* of *Vampire Academy*.

This is Richelle's child, not my child . . . I am simply the friendly guidance counselor helping the child grow up (or grow down) into being a movie. But . . . if I get the chance to tackle the second book, *Frostbite* . . . there are matters I'd like to explore pertaining to the evolution of the Strigoi.

Q: Were there any surprises you encountered while working on the script?

One of the big surprises when I sat down to write was how many scenes were described by Rose without any dialogue.

Daniel Waters, Zoey Deutch & Mark Waters give *Vampire Academy* a thumbs-up.

Moments such as Rose telling Dimitri and Kirova about Lissa's cutting, and Rose investigating old books with Christian, were mostly internalized by Rose. When people come at me with, "How dare you! That line of dialogue was not in the book," I've got a defense. Nobody wants to watch a film with wall-to-wall narration, so I was going to have to be more than a typist in translating the book into a script.

More personally, I was surprised how much music affected my writing of this. When I was faltering, my playlist would bring me back to life. I could not have adapted *Vampire Academy* without "Dreams so Real" by Metric, "Sinful Nature" by Bear in Heaven, and "Perfectly Flawed" by Otep.

Q: Were there many rewrites happening on set? What kinds of things might warrant changes on the go?

If you look at the poster of *Vampire Academy* and know anything about Hollywood, you'll notice there are some names of very volatile people with big personalities associated with this film. Forty-eight hours before we began shooting, something remarkable happened—everyone was happy with the script. So much blood, sweat, and tears had gone into that last draft that I think everyone was scared to mess with it. When

you finally lift off the runway, nobody wants to re-land the plane.

Sure, we re-modulated some words from our beloved Russian, but here's what you have to remember: My brother was a premed student when he first visited one of my sets, and he got so angry at the way my script was being massacred that he left the medical path to become a director who makes more money than me. Mark is always willing to try new things, but he is a mammoth protector of my words. If you're going to improvise, it better be good.

Now, my dialogue is a little untraditional . . . it's not "the way teenagers really talk." My gods are Shakespeare and Turner Classic Movies . . . but it turns out most young actors *love* to be challenged and don't really want to "talk the way teenagers really talk." Our goal was always to make the odd seem natural, rather than changing every third word to *awesome* and *sick*.

Now it's going to be tragic and hilarious when I read other people's answers to this question and they say, "Oh yeah, we changed everything."

Q: What is your relationship like with Richelle? Did you have long talks about the characters and story before you began working? Did she offer any insight to help your process?

I did not meet with Richelle before writing, I did not speak with her before writing, I did not ask questions of her before writing. Richelle communicated that she knows the difference between a novel and a screenplay . . . but let me tell you, the weekend when she finally did read the script was quite suspenseful!

Here's the great thing about Richelle: There was a commercial back in the day where the guy says, "I'm not only the president of the Hair Club for Men, I'm also a member," and then he reveals his baldness. Richelle is not just the creator of *Vampire Academy*, but she is a true, warm, and utterly engaged fan as well. She read the script with wonder and excitement, not with her arms crossed and a sour "you better not screw this up" expression on her face. She did not go through the script with a microscope and a clipboard, drearily tabulating, "In the book, it was like this . . . but now in the script, it's like this . . ." Richelle let herself experience her own work in a new way (I recently had a similar epiphany watching a fantastic musical version of *Heathers*). Now if Richelle could only get her most rabid fans to have the same attitude!

In all seriousness, as I hinted before, Richelle has a strong—the strongest—sense of what the soul of *Vampire Academy* is. For instance, I turned Lissa's literal "cutting" from the novel into something she does telekinetically, so when I finally did meet Richelle, I thought she was going to throw coffee in my face. But it was one of the

first things she brought up—she liked that I took away the afterschool-special nature of self-mutilation and put it in the realm of fantasy/allegory.

My brother and I did not get away completely scot-free . . . When we contemplated making Jesse of Latin descent and Christian into a blond . . . well, that's when the coffee started flying across the table!

Q: Which of the actors do you feel was cast to perfection based on your vision of the script?

When Danny DeVito read my first draft of *Batman Returns*, he was a little glum and disappointed. He said, "You wrote a Danny DeVito part." Ever since then, I never try to overimagine who should play a character and what they should look like.

I have invented a word for the cast of *Vampire Academy*: "berfect," meaning better than perfect. I was sure we'd end up casting some anorexic fashion model as Lissa, but the part is now unimaginable as anyone but Lucy Fry. Her constant optimism and wonder put a smile on every beleaguered crew member's face. She is truly a princess

Rose provides comfort to a troubled Lissa.

Mark Waters and Daniel Waters chat casually with First Assistant Director Toby Ford.

worth dying for. Dimitri and Danila are both Russian, both handsome, but Danila is such a hilarious, lovable goofball that I never thought he could be the serious, stoic guardian of the novel. But not only does he nail the serious, he does it with a twinkle in his eye that makes the part that much more entertaining.

And then there's Zoey . . . At this point, I don't honestly know where Rose ends and Zoey begins and vice versa. I knew Zoey before the movie as the best friend of my best friend's daughter (Zoey and I are both Scorpios born on November 10, which says a lot about our snarky, outrageous bond), and even as a child, she had an attitude of "shock first, ask questions later." Zoey's attitude was never a problem; there was worry that she could not properly kick ass. Asses were properly kicked.

That all said, our redheads, Cameron Monaghan as Rose's dhampir buddy, Mason, and Claire Foy as the mad but noble Ms. Karp . . . come on, if anybody was picturing anything different from them, I don't know what book they were reading, but it sure was not *Vampire Academy*.

Q: When writing action sequences, how do you reconcile the many aspects of postproduction F/X and such? Are these things decided ahead of time and worked into the script?

Producers and directors kind of hate screenwriters because our process occurs alone in a room in our underwear, letting our imaginations run wild without a care in the world. A writer can't spend time scanning the price of a fantasy. I naturally assume everything is going to look amazing and awe-inspiring. I have no interest in seeing how the sausage is made in the back of the kitchen.

I knew going in we did not have *Batman* or *Superman* money to make the first *Vampire Academy*, but I also knew that most of the first novel is character- and mystery-based. Hopefully this one will be successful enough to afford all those Strigoi attacks in *Shadow Kiss*!

But I will say not a day went by without my brother sneering about "those [insert expletive adjective here] *psi-hounds*!" Richelle created them, I embellished them, but to actually bring them to life . . . well, that's why I stay out of the kitchen.

Absolutely both. My brother is not on Facebook. My brother has not checked out any of the *Vampire Academy* websites. My brother doesn't know what a Tumblr is. My brother is a very lucky guy! I read e-v-e-r-y-t-h-i-n-g and take it all way too seriously.

As you point out, I'm answering this question just after the release of the teaser and man, I don't think footage has been this analyzed since the Zapruder film. The response has been so insanely passionate and passionately insane that I have to lie down just rethinking about it.

Now, a mature adult mind would say, "Dan, calm down, these silly teenagers are judging the entire film on the basis of one minute of marketing . . ." But as it has been established, my brother took most of the mature genes in the family. Deep down, I know managing pre-release expectations through social media is a game I can't win, so I shouldn't be playing. However, it's only by reading it all that I can see just how truly wacky and contradictory all the hype and antihype is. Apparently the cast is both too young and too old, too skinny, too fat, too CW/MTV, not CW/MTV enough, wrong hair, wrong dress, wrong stake, wrong eyewear ("Natalie doesn't wear glasses!" "Hey, you try to make Sarah Hyland look unhot!").

My rule from the beginning with *Vampire Academy* is to listen to the fans, respect the fans, but don't be their bitch. The version in a reader's mind is always the best one—it is not affected by budget, weather . . . you can switch out daydream actors from scene to scene . . . How can I compete? My job is to make a great movie that also appeals to at least some of the billions of people who haven't even heard of *Vampire Academy* . . . not just a C-Span reading of the book. This means increasing the mystery elements beyond Rose's inner-voice narration and adding more action (Rose has a lot more game against the guardians early on, and our villains have got more up their sleeve than a couple psi-hounds!).

The irony is that the teasers, trailers, and commercials are going to be judged in a harsher light than the actual movie. That's why my brother has not let himself be distracted by social media—because the goal all along has been that once we lock the readers into the roller coaster that is the movie, they won't be able to stop and replay it every three seconds to reconsult the book with a flashlight . . . There will be bumps along the way, but hopefully the ultimate effect at the very end will be pure exhilaration and giddiness at how we honored the original book.

When I was a kid, I went to the movie *Jaws* after reading the book, which I adored. I came out of the film blown away . . . Only later did I realize, "Hey, what happened to the affair between the sheriff's wife and the Richard Dreyfuss character?" I hope I can create the same temporary amnesia.

Only adapt novels into movies that everyone hates! Just kidding . . . kind of.

ZOEY DEUTCH AS
Rose Hathaway

Zoey Deutch may be young, but she's no stranger to the entertainment business. Having grown up watching her mother, Lea Thompson, act in films like *Back to the Future*, and her father, Howard Deutch, direct films like *Pretty in Pink*, Zoey no doubt developed a keen eye and an artistic sensibility from a very early age. As a girl she studied dance and eventually graduated from the Los Angeles County High School for the Arts after majoring in theater and visual arts. From there she began on the path to success, landing roles in the indie film *Mayor Cupcake*, as well as TV shows like *The Suite Life on Deck*, *NCIS*, and *Ringer*. But it wasn't until her starring role as Emily Asher in the film *Beautiful Creatures*, based on the top-selling book series, that Hollywood stood up and took note. Her performance didn't go unnoticed by the producers of *Vampire Academy*, and she soon found herself cast in the role of Rose Hathaway, Lissa Dragomir's strong-willed guardian who'd do absolutely anything to protect her best friend. Just as fans connected with the intense and emotional

Natalie Dashkov, Lissa Dragomir, and Rose Hathaway nervously make their way into the dance hall.

"I love that *Vampire Academy* is a coming-of-age story, a story of friendship between two best friends. I also love that there is a sense of humor about the world of the film. You root for these characters like crazy till the bitter end, but there are still laughs throughout the whole journey."

—ZOEY DEUTCH

friendship between these two women, so did Deutch. In Rose, Richelle Mead created a character who could inspire you to be a better friend, surprise you with a witty retort, and ultimately kick your butt if you messed with her. It was a role that Deutch found she could sink her teeth into.

"I connected with Rose's humor as a means of survival, her hotheadedness and passion, and her fiercely loyal nature toward those she loves," Deutch confessed. "Rose Hathaway's sense of humor is as brutal as her fighting skills. She's someone who I, Zoey Deutch, would not want to mess with. I connected with her being passionate and not holding back her feelings. Rose's motivation throughout the story is rooted in protecting Lissa, but progressively she gains more desire to be the best protector she can be, and therefore has more confidence in her ability. Of course, there are many other motivations strewn throughout, including her big fat crush on Dimitri, her want for her mother's approval, and her love of knowing everything that's going on around her. My favorite thing about how Richelle Mead wrote the characters of *Vampire Academy* is

that they're all playing against type. For example, Natalie is thought to be a meek and innocent Moroi, when really she is the most vindictive and cunning person in the story. Also, Mason is written as the dorky boy stuck in the friend zone, but in reality he's a killing machine with tons of confidence, enough to chase after Rose like he does. In addition, Lissa is thought to be a sort of helpless and fragile creature, when really she's wielding more power than anyone else at St. Vlad's. These walking contradictions are what make these characters so interesting to play, to read, and to watch."

Rose's guardian training pays off.

Preparing for the role meant not only decoding the script but absorbing the mythology established within the *Vampire Academy* universe. Fortunately Deutch was able to tackle the challenge early on in the experience. "The only time I had trouble wrapping my head around the mythology was during the audition process, just because the vocabulary of it was so new to me," she explained. "I really wanted the part, and I remember trying to remember dhampir, Moroi, Strigoi, molnija marks, St. Vlad's, etc., and feeling like I might have a stroke."

Daniel Waters's screenplay drew rave reviews from the creative team and was met with equal excitement from Deutch as she delved deeper into Rose's humor and truth. "Initially I was struck by how funny the script was. In my opinion, you don't read a lot of young-adult adaptations that actually capture the hilarity of being a teenager. Also, as a woman, I deeply appreciated the fact that this is a story that puts friendship before romance. And, of course, I couldn't deny the fact that Rose's dialogue felt like

things coming out of my own crazy head—I immediately knew who she was."

As shooting began, Deutch dove into the experience headfirst, despite a handful of initial complications. "The first day of filming was very exciting in a sort of 'not really' way because I had an eye infection, and Mark Waters had to shoot my back the entire day because of it. Some of my finest 'backting,'" she divulged. But production had only just begun, and there were plenty of thrilling moments ahead. "I was super excited to shoot the charm necklace scene, the fight scene with Mason in training, and the last scene of the movie. But the ones that ended up being my favorite to shoot, if I *had* to pick, were a library scene with Christian, a small scene with Dimitri walking back from training, and a flashback scene with Ms. Karp."

Long hours on set might seem like the kind of thing that would aggravate and annoy a costar, but not in the case of Lucy Fry. These two young women were able to use their experiences on and off set to

further solidify their union and bond them as blood sisters.

"Of course my bond with Zoey was the deepest because we worked with each other every day under a huge range of emotional and physical conditions," Fry explained. "Going through the journey together created a real-life bond. She has such a bright energy that could light up the whole set; I loved working with her." But in the end, the ultimate blessing came from author Richelle Mead herself, who gave Zoey Deutch's performance this glowing review:

"I think Zoey Deutch has got the spirit and the personality of Rose. I mean, obviously, the thing with actors is they take on roles. They're not exactly like the characters they play in real life. But

at the same time, there's an energy about Zoey, the actress, that resonates with the character. Mark Waters was talking about when she auditioned, when she walked in, people were like, 'Oh my God, that's her.' She carries it. I love following her on Twitter. There's a spirit of adventure in her. There are these pictures she tweeted—she and Cameron Monaghan [who plays Mason] got stuck on the Tube. They started doing backflips off the side because they were bored, and they were stuck in there, and

it was really funny, and it was cute, the pictures they tweeted there. It's that fun and that energy that just comes through as Rose . . . [And] she just threw herself into [the training]. It's a very physical role. She was with a trainer full days, multiple times a week, just driving her body, making sure she was in the best shape she could be to carry out Rose. I think that's what really defines the character. She looks like the part, to me, as well, but it's so much more than having a facial resemblance to the character. You've got to be able to portray them. That's what everyone was looking at when they cast her, and I think they did it beautifully."[12]

"I think that a lot of people like how in control she is. And even in regard to sex, it's not callous or something she necessarily treats lightly. I think that's what's key. It's not someone who gets used or isn't thoughtful about her sexuality. She very much is and I think that's the important part of being strong about it, being decisive and knowing what you will do and what you won't do. And I think that was the most important piece to care about with that."[13]

ROSE AND LISSA: *Blood Sisters*

"There were three sides of Rose's connection to Lissa that I was excited to play out. The first were the action-heavy sequences, which put on display just how far Rose will go to protect Lissa. And my favorite scene would be running away from the guards sent from St. Vladimir's at the beginning of the movie. Second were the moments where Lissa breaks down and you see a very gentle and maternal side of Rose emerge. And thirdly, 'Lissavision.' It was fun to play with Rose's internal struggle of knowing she's looking in on something she shouldn't, but also can't stop it from happening. Lucy and I grew incredibly close. She has a bright spirit, and energy you just want to be around. She lights up a room when she walks in. We hung out in L.A. a bit prior to shipping out to London, and then spent two weeks rehearsing with one another before the film. Lucy makes me want to be a better person."—Zoey Deutch on the relationship between Rose and Lissa

"Before we started filming, Zoey and I got to know each other in L.A. and discussed Rose and Lissa's relationship and how we wanted to play it. Somehow, our on-screen relationship melted into everyday life. We always felt quite protective of each other. Zoey was the strong guardian, so she would be really bold in fighting to stick up for me. We were always there for each other. I really enjoyed every scene between Rose and Lissa because there is no holding back in their relationship. I was excited to film their fight scenes because the characters have such a deep bond that we could let go and fight like siblings. Zoey and I were both excited to play Rose and Lissa's offbeat sense of humor. I think it perfectly captured the way a best friendship develops strange personal jokes and a way of interacting that is different from an everyday friendship. And, like Rose and Lissa, we could be our goofiest selves with each other."—Lucy Fry on her friendship with Zoey Deutch and their bond as Rose and Lissa

LUCY FRY AS *Lissa Dragomir*

"Lucy is the sweetest, most gentle human being I've ever met. Other than the fact that she's a tomboy, she really is Lissa, so it's perfect. We had a friendship in real life that I'm pretty sure translates to screen."
—Sarah Hyland on Lucy Fry

Australian actress Lucy Fry may be unfamiliar to American audiences, but all that is poised to change when *Vampire Academy* hits movie screens in 2014. Fry is no stranger to the realm of fantasy. She's best known for her role as Zoey in the teen drama *Lightning Point*, an Australian television show that followed a pair of

alien girls stranded on Earth and learning to cope with their new surroundings. Her role as the Moroi vampire princess Lissa Dragomir in *Vampire Academy* marks her big-screen debut and is sure to have people talking. As with any professional experience, Fry threw herself into researching Lissa's world. Unsurprisingly, her first stop was the first Vampire Academy novel.

"I read the first book about five times while I was preparing for the role. I really wanted to completely embody Lissa and, naturally, the book gave me a much deeper psychological and emotional insight into Lissa than the script. A script is action-based, while a book delves into emotions. I didn't read ahead before filming because I didn't want to know what happens to Lissa before she knows. I wanted to go through the journey with her. It was so hard to resist! Now that we have just finished book/film number one, I am greedily reading on to the second . . . and I doubt I'll be able to stop myself this time." And what about all the jargon and mythology? For Fry it was smooth sailing. "What mythology? It's

Lissa prepares to feed.

the truth! I love the sense of wonderment and mystery that comes from an unknown world. I was so excited to make a film where the rules of everyday life were absurd compared with the human world. I love the absurdity." Before she landed the role, however, Fry was able to connect to the material through her real-life adventures. "I first read the script when I was backpacking through Europe with one of my best friends, so its focus on friendship felt connected to my experiences at the time. I loved the offbeat sense of humor. There are a lot of vampire interpretations out there, but this is the only one I have come across that offsets the action and mystery with a vibrant, playful quirkiness. I remember preparing for my audition on the plane to L.A.—I was drawing all these weird vampire pictures and I am sure the gorgeous lady next to me thought I was very odd."

Though her work was a source of inspiration, Richelle Mead was unable to speak at length with Fry and her fellow cast members about the characters they were portraying. But Mead's presence was felt on set and her words of encouragement meant a great deal to Fry, as the young actress faced the role of a lifetime. "As soon as I found out I got the part I couldn't wait to meet Richelle and ask her about Lissa," Fry explained. "Unfortunately we only met her toward the end of filming, so by then I had already created my interpretation of Lissa.

Lissa shares a look with Queen Tatiana.

However, every word she wrote about Lissa in the book I highlighted and analyzed and interpreted until I felt like I'd completely absorbed her. So Richelle gave me insights through the pages of her book. I cried when I found out that she told the producers that I was her dream Lissa. It meant the world to me."

As filming began and Fry went deeper inside her character's head, she felt inspired and embraced the emotional bond between Lissa and Rose—that is, the heart of the film. "This is a story I would love to tell because of the extraordinary friendship between Rose and Lissa," she stated. "I loved the humor, the action, the romance, the powers, and most of all the friendship that overcame every challenge. I connected the most with Lissa's sensitivity.

Lissa absorbs the energy around her like a sponge. That is one of the reasons that she is so deeply affected by seeing other beings in pain, and has the power to heal with her spirit. Of course I don't have the power of spirit, but sometimes I struggle with absorbing the energy of others. By experiencing Lissa's journey, I learned more about managing my own sensitivity. Lissa is motivated by the desire to feel safe. She has lost her whole family, has been running away from an unknown threat for two years, Rose is the only person she trusts, and she is battling emotional instability from her powers. So due to these circumstances, Lissa's longing to feel safe drives her actions through the entire film. This is evident in her friendship with Rose, as her guardian; in her relationship with Christian, who calms her nervous energy; in her manipulation of the high-school royals, to protect herself from their bullying. Of course, as the last

remaining member of the royal Dragomir bloodline . . . Lissa's dream to feel safe is not an easy thing to reach."

There were long hours during the *Vampire Academy* shoot, but it was actually Fry's first day on set that would be one of her most memorable . . . and most intimidating. "On the first day, I was so nervous I almost vomited. I was also incredibly excited. Thankfully the food stayed down—that would not have been a good first impression! It was a huge ballroom scene with lots of dynamic relationships and action segments. I was amazed by the way Mark navigated this complicated scene—he coordinated amazing tracking shots following the girls through the party, and created a beautiful flow between the various actions. Mark's measured direction made me feel much more relaxed, and I loved the way he experimented with the various ways to play each scene. Every take, he would direct the actors to try the scene with a different tone, which allowed some really surprising and interesting undercurrents to happen. I entered the day feeling terrified, and by the end of the day I felt calmly reassured to be working with someone so thorough and with such amazing attention to detail."

Fry did the creative legwork to fully understand Lissa's motivations, allowing the actress to portray the character

Lucy Fry takes a peek through the camera between setups.

honestly, but sometimes it was the little unexpected things that brought about her biggest breakthroughs. "Something that surprised me was how hard it is to see with green eye contacts in," she admitted. "It could be quite hard to connect to reality sometimes with this blurry green sheen on everything. That was my biggest challenge on set, overcoming the green to connect to the scene. Though sometimes the 'blurry' world I saw helped me to connect to Lissa's 'blurry' emotional state. After Mark's advice, I learned to work with blurry."

Though she may be green to the film world, Lucy Fry understands and respects the strange bit of kismet that brought her into the *Vampire Academy* fold. The opportunity to play a character with as much depth and emotional resonance as Lissa Dragomir doesn't come along every day. But it's more than just luck that earned her the role; it was hard work, determination, and good old-fashioned talent. Fry knows this fact and is thankful.

"This film is unique because it is cheeky and playful, but is set in a dark and mysterious aesthetic. I have heard people say it is *Harry Potter* meets *Twilight* meets *Mean Girls* . . . which is certainly a combination that has never been done before. The mythology of this vampire world is different to the usual vampire film. The relationship between the Moroi, dhampirs, and the Strigoi creates an exciting tension that usually only exists between vampires and humans. It allows the action to happen in a world that is completely hidden from the human eye. Playing Lissa was the most thrilling, terrifying, uplifting, fulfilling, surprising, and expansive experience of my life so far. I was a little hippie on a world backpacking adventure, and suddenly I became a vampire princess. I still find it hard to believe that it is real. I feel ludicrously lucky to have been chosen to play such a compassionate, complex character for my first film, and I am so grateful to all the beautiful people who made it possible for me. It was a dream come true. I felt like Cinderella every day, going to work with this amazing team on this dream script. If Cinderella were a vampire."

> "As soon as we finished filming, I felt like I had been woken up from a magical dream and had to pinch myself to remember that it was real. Every scene is now a blur. So I feel like I will be watching it for the first time with the rest of the world. I am nervous. But excited."
>
> — LUCY FRY

DANILA KOZLOVSKY AS *Dimitri Belikov*

Dimitri Belikov is a fierce, protective guardian of the Moroi, and a man who chooses his words carefully. It's a description that could also be used for Danila Kozlovsky, the actor who portrays him . . . except, of course, the guardian part. But that could be true as well because he's *just that good*. Kozlovsky has an air of mystery and unpredictability about him that fans will no doubt find captivating in his role as Lissa Dragomir's newly appointed protector. Kozlovsky flexed his acting muscles to bring Dimitri's stoic, protective nature to life, but there's more to this Russian bruiser than meets the eye. He also doubles as Rose Hathaway's conflicted love interest, a man sworn to his duty who finds himself falling for a girl, despite serious reservations.

Vampire Academy casting director Marci Liroff saw something incredibly special in Kozlovsky, which ultimately landed him the coveted role. "A casting colleague of mine who we worked with on *Mean Girls*, Susan Shopmaker, sent me Danila's picture, along with several other Russian and eastern European actors she had found online," Liroff explained. "As soon as I saw his picture my heart skipped a beat. He was hard to reach, as he was either finishing a film or promoting a film and doing a lot of theater at the time. I finally got in touch with his agent, Richard Cook, in Ireland, and we set about trying to get Danila together with Mark Waters on Skype so they could record his audition. When we got the audition link, I started watching it in my office and started screaming, 'Oh

my God! Oh my God!' Then I heard my associate Michelle in her office screaming, 'Oh my God! Oh my God!' Then I sent it to the producer's assistant, Soumya, and I heard her from upstairs screaming, 'Oh my God! Oh my God!' Then we started doing the 'Danila dance' because we just knew. We just knew. Danila's charisma is off the charts. He's also a total goofball, which we probably won't see in this film because Dimitri is so dark and brooding. This role will make him a superstar in America."

After being cast, Kozlovsky jumped right into the character, absorbing Mead's initial tale and relishing every word of screenwriter Daniel Waters's film script. "There were no problems wrapping my head around the mythology of the books," Kozlovsky explained. "I accepted the author's world immediately. It was amazingly written and creative, an unusual and interesting story with much humor. I was able to meet Richelle, but unfortunately we had no opportunity to speak personally about Dimitri; but she gave me lots of ideas and insight from her books about Dimitri's character. And my first impression after reading Daniel

Danila Kozlovsky, Sarah Hyland, and Deepak Nayar applaud a job well done.

Waters's film script was, 'Wow, it's great!' It was interesting and I liked it very much. It was humorous, and I felt it had a good story line. There were interesting and positive relationships between characters

and a unique love affair between Rose and Dimitri. I was excited about everything that was connected to that relationship." As for similarities between the actor and his guardian character, Kozlovsky found just two. "Russian nationality," he stated. "And I like old music." But there was definitely more to Dimitri than met the eye, and Kozlovsky was keen to focus on the character's drive and complexity. "Dimitri always gives one hundred percent, and encourages others to do the same, teaching people how to survive and how to help Moroi survive. He's also motivated by love and caring and wants to help Rose control her emotions, to become more mature, to be more responsible. In the meantime, Dimitri is falling in love with Rose and losing control because of love."

Despite his lengthy film résumé, Kozlovsky had yet to shoot beyond his homeland and was anxious to embark on a new adventure. "It was my first experience working outside of Russia. I was very nervous and concerned because it was a totally new experience for me, but at the same time I was very excited and honored to work with these people. I was overwhelmed with emotions when production was finished. I was very honored to play the role and work with the fantastic Mr. Waters."

"I'm afraid Dimitri came straight outta my brain. People have asked if someone inspired his creation and I have contemplated that maybe I should have mentioned it a long time ago, come up with a story to stick to and tell people. I can make up this great thing about maybe my car broke down and a hot Russian came and helped me fix my tire. I basically built a lot of mystique around the character. But I'm afraid the truth is he was born straight from me."[14]

After incredibly long days and many months of shooting, Kozlovsky got to know his costars Lucy Fry and Zoey Deutch quite well, and praised their professionalism and talent. "Lucy and I became very good friends on the set. We used film language in daily conversation; for example, I called her 'Royal Highness' and she answered, 'Yes, my guardian,'" he explained. "Zoey and I also became close friends and had a lot of fun on and off the set. It was incredible; she has amazing talent, she is gorgeous, a true professional, and a very good friend. It was very interesting and memorable working for the first time with American and English people. I will never forget my first experience. They were very friendly and open." With so many fond memories, Kozlovsky found it difficult to choose just one, but was able instead to offer a handful of meaningful moments that held a special place in his heart. "My favorite moments are the love-charm scene and the final conversation with Rose. I also liked the training scene with Rose. Something else that I found interesting was the bonding relationship between Lissa and Christian. It intrigued me because I could relate to their loneliness and loss of parents. I sympathized with their personal situation and the challenges they faced from the other students. They had the courage to stay together despite the gossip and backstabbing that occurred."

After wrapping the production, Kozlovsky was excited to have had the opportunity to bring Dimitri to the big screen, and found peace with his place in the *Vampire Academy* world. "I use criticism as a positive motivator, in spite of the negativism," he explained. "I want to thank all the fans for the amazing support they showed us during the filming. I hope they will continue to support this release as well as future endeavors. I worry about their reactions to my work and to our movie," he confessed. "But I can't wait for the fans to see this movie, and their reaction." Upon further reflection, Kozlovsky was also thankful to be a part of such a respected creative team, though the high quality of the production was something of a shock to his system. "I was surprised by the

Zoey Deutch gives Danila Kozlovsky a playful peck on the cheek.

professionalism and work ethic of the cast and crew," he admitted. But even the little things filled the newly minted star with both wonder and delight. "The breakfast was also kind of a surprise. I wasn't expecting so many eggs and salmon."

"Dimitri, I love, and I love Danila's portrayal of him. So brooding and serious, but also passionate. Amazing. And Danila is truly awesome."—Dominic Sherwood on Danila Kozlovsky

"Danila and I had the luxury of being able to train together in both L.A. and London long before shooting began. It was great because we built a rapport in the gym that was reflected in all the training scenes.

In terms of the romantic aspect of Rose and Dimitri's relationship . . . like, um, sorry, not difficult to be in love with him. Everyone should be a little bit more like Danila."—Zoey Deutch on Danila Kozlovsky

"Dimitri really intrigued me because his relationship with Lissa is completely unspoken. They only say about two words to each other throughout the whole film! Danila and I would joke about how we can't talk on-screen. Lissa only sees Dimitri in guardian mode, and I felt intrigued to know more about who he is underneath that, especially because of Rose's crush on him!"—Lucy Fry on Lissa's relationship with Dimitri

RICHELLE MEAD ON HER FAVORITE SCENE BETWEEN *Dimitri and Rose*

"I am excited for all of them. Really, I just want to see them together. I think Zoey and Danila are such amazing casting choices for it. And they get along great offscreen as well, which I think is fun. I love that everyone working on the movie is having such a good time with it. There are so many great scenes in the evolution of Rose and Dimitri's relationship. I know that the love-charm scene is the big, hot one that people are excited about. I'm excited for that too, but even just their initial meeting, which is done really well in the script—you know, where they had this standoff in the beginning—is just powerful as well. You know, where they are sizing each other up. You know, she's this reckless, scrappy fighter girl, and here he is, a seasoned, calm veteran. There is power in that. I am just . . . any of it, I am overjoyed to see."[15]

DOMINIC SHERWOOD AS *Christian Ozera*

Christian Ozera's past is dark. His parents became murderous Strigoi when he was just a child, and ever since then he began building walls between himself and the outside world. Emotionally, he masked his pain with arrogance and refused to let himself be controlled. But attending St. Vladimir's Academy and meeting Lissa Dragomir changed all of that. Suddenly he was swept away in a drama much bigger than himself. Christian was exactly the kind of character that actor Dominic Sherwood was excited to tackle. Though, as Sherwood is quick to point out, he's nothing like his character all. Okay . . . maybe just a little.

"I'm not much like Christian. I have been known to be a little sarcastic (maybe a lot sarcastic) at times," he confided. "But that's really the only similarity." Playing a character with depth is always a welcome reward for an actor, but the material also intrigued Sherwood because, despite the supernatural aspects, the film's themes echoed real-world situations. "It was interesting to see a completely surreal world that also had vast elements of everything normal people struggle with—bullying, teasing, etc.—at high school. That's what first grabbed me: the paradoxical nature of the screenplay. I think the mythology is made a lot easier because these kids are dealing with everyday problems as well as life-threatening ones." Sherwood also found that the material retained its authenticity, melding seamlessly with the arcane. "We deal with the supernatural in a much more mature way than may have been done before. We cover sexuality and violence and

peril to swing the audiences open to not just the younger but also more adult."

Though Sherwood read the initial *Vampire Academy* novel after booking the role, his review of the second and subsequent novels remains a slow-going process. "I don't want to get too ahead of myself," he confessed. "One small step at a time." But reading Mead's first exploration of Christian Ozera was enough to hook Sherwood, and he was able to capture exactly what makes the conflicted Ozera tick. "At the beginning, he kind of hates everyone because of how they treated him. Again, it's very high school behavior for a very supernatural reason, but he falls in love and his motives change through the beautiful Lissa. I was most excited about doing the scenes I auditioned with. I auditioned six times for *Vampire Academy*, so it was a hell of a process, and every time, it was the same few scenes in the attic, though my favorite moment in the script was anything with fire magic." Unsurprisingly, Sherwood has nothing but positive reviews for his co-stars. "The first day of filming was the Equinox Dance, and Lucy and I were kind of thrown into it. But it is so easy to work with her that I never felt uneasy. We didn't really need to talk at all, it just happened. It was amazing. I had butterflies. The whole cast was there, two-hundred-plus extras. And it was a ball,

truly an amazing first few days. Lucy and Zoey are both amazing and they quickly became some of my favorite people. They both have an amazing ability to make me smile, which I love, and both are so unbelievably talented."

Sarah Hyland, who plays Natalie Dashkov, developed her own on-set friendship with Sherwood and had an interesting observation about her character's relationship with Christian Ozera.

"Me and Dom would joke around a lot on set and off set that Natalie and Christian are always alone," Hyland recalled. "Rose and Lissa would always leave me sitting by myself, and Christian, of course, would be way in the back by himself. So why shouldn't Christian and Natalie be friends, or at least sit near each other so they'd have someone to talk to . . . But I think Christian would get fed up with Natalie's gabbing; he'd probably set her on fire."

Though he was unable to meet Richelle Mead during her set visit, Sherwood describes her as "a lovely and very passionate woman. It's very nice to have someone so influential, but also so supportive, behind you." Despite a handful of appearances on British television, *Vampire Academy* was Sherwood's first film venture. The experience satiated the actor's thirst for the unknown, and he assures viewers that there's plenty of excitement just around the corner. "There were lots of surprises, but it's always best just to roll with them. What excites me most about the film? All of it. There aren't any boring moments."

"I could always count on Dom to make fun of me and vice versa, which I think is because we're such good friends; we feel we can do that. I think?"—Zoey Deutch on Dominic Sherwood

Sarah Hyland has a confession to make.

"I've been a bad girl. I've only read the first Vampire Academy book," the actress admitted, then quickly defended herself. "But that's because it's the only one that Natalie is in." Forgivable transgressions aside, Hyland has been acting in television and film since a very young age and has no doubt done her research when it comes to playing Natalie Dashkov. A social recluse, the mousy Dashkov has some secrets that could seriously threaten the balance at St. Vladimir's Academy. It gave Hyland a chance to dive into the realm of fantasy, something she hadn't had an opportunity to do before. "I loved the script and I loved this new world of vampires. It wasn't like *Twilight*, but it wasn't like *True Blood*. It was completely new, and that is was I loved most about it. I love fantasy books. Whether it's wizards (huge *Harry Potter* geek), zombies, vampires, kings and queens with dragons—I'm into it. So it was amazing to be able to learn about this whole new world."

Hyland knew the role wasn't exactly the type that people expected her to play. The challenge excited the actress and made her layer the moments in her performance with character flourishes in order to keep people guessing. "I gave Natalie these little 'quirks,'" Hyland explained. "She scrunches up her face a lot with her glasses, almost always has her mouth open, and does these weird hand movements. I'm a bit spastic . . . only every once and a while, but I found myself turning more and more into Natalie as shooting progressed. I became so clumsy I was almost hopeless. Natalie, in the end, is a daddy's girl; she would do anything for him. There's definitely a dark side to her; she has a very strange fascination with boys. There are some moments where the audience will see

mysterious case that I'd love to solve."

Hyland is no stranger to cast bonding, having recently entered her fifth season as Haley Dunphy on the critically acclaimed TV show *Modern Family*. But being on a film set with a cast made up of other young professionals became quite a comfort during the long shoot. "Being on set for the first time was like the first day at school. We had all had a cast dinner and went out afterward a couple days before filming, so we knew each other, but we all really bonded on those first few days of shooting. It was the dance, so all the students and guardians (plus around two hundred background) were there and we really got to know one another. Everyone got so close while filming. Every weekend we would all get together and go out and have the best time. Zoey and I became really close and are still really great friends to this day. We're so alike in the way we go about things . . . and being really loud and stupid . . . that's mainly what attracted us to each other. But in all seriousness, she's a phenomenal person and an amazing talent. Dom, Ed, Chris, Lucy, Danila, Cam, and Dominique were also so much fun to be around. I really fell in love with the entire cast; we would go to dinners and paint the town red. I was very sad that everyone else would be coming back for a second time around (hopefully), but I loved the character of Natalie so much that I wouldn't have had it any other way. I'm so lucky to have been a part of this movie and created such amazing friendships."

Natalie go dark for like a second and come right back into her sweet, naive self. I hope those moments make it in. Richelle Mead came to set closer to the end of filming, so I had already come up with my little quirks for Natalie and didn't want to ask Richelle about her. I was so afraid if I did that she would give me an answer that I had been doing six weeks of Natalie all wrong."

Despite falling in love with Natalie and her mysterious motives, Hyland was also taken with Rose Hathaway and saw something new and unexpected in the character. "I loved Rose and how she was so independent and had a fierce loyalty to those close to her; she wasn't a damsel in distress, that's for sure. It also has this sexy edginess to it, which I feel is very different from what's been done before. And I want to learn even more about Sonya Karp. She's a

"I look up to Sarah Hyland, as such a professional and a lovely person to be around."

—ZOEY DEUTCH ON SARAH HYLAND

SAMI GAYLE AS *Mia Rinaldi*

What exactly does it take to be a villain in a world of bloodthirsty vampires? Sami Gayle might just have the answer. As St. Vladimir's resident troublemaker, Mia Rinaldi, Gayle had a chance to play a character whose bad behavior masks a bigger mystery. Having appeared previously on the TV show *Blue Bloods*, *Vampire Academy* marks an all-new chapter in Gayle's promising career on-screen.

Q: What was your first impression after reading the script? What did you find interesting about the world of *Vampire Academy*?

My first impression after reading the script was, "I have to be a part of this crazy world!" The script was packed with sassy humor, sophistication, blazing romance, and an air of mystery that immensely attracted me to the project. I loved that all of the characters were so entrenched in the vampiric world and that behind their supernatural characteristics, all of the students and professors at St. Vladimir's Academy were real people that an audience could truly relate to. After all, everyone knows a Mia Rinaldi, the unpopular-girl-turned-popular-princess who is always in

everyone's business but is actually just hiding her insecurities.

Q: What did you feel were the most interesting aspects of Mia's personality and motivation?

What I loved about Mia was that her catty, busybody, mean attitude was really just an act that masked her insecurity of being from a less renowned, working-class family compared to the family of Princess Vasilisa Dragomir. It was difficult for me to honestly portray Mia, thinking of her as a vampire, as I had no idea of what it would be like to be a vampire. But when I

began looking at Mia as an insecure girl who was putting on a tough face to cover up her fear of losing her boyfriend and "queen bee" position at the school to Vasilisa Dragomir, I began to understand Mia very deeply and was able to become her. It was important for me to look at Mia as a normal human being, rather than as this supernatural creature. The fact that Mia is a vampire, and that I got to fang, was just the icing on the cake!

Q: What were your first impressions when you stepped onto the *Vampire Academy* set for the first time?

I got the greatest rush stepping on set for the first time. The first day we shot, we filmed the dance scene and the entire cast was present. It was surreal to see all of the characters I had been imagining from the script and the novels come to life. The cast of actors in this film is so diverse and beautiful. The sets were extravagant and magical, but would you really expect anything else at St. Vladimir's Academy? We were shooting nights, so I became nocturnal. I actually felt like I was a vampire attending the school, which made becoming Mia much easier.

Q: Have you read the Vampire Academy books? If so, did you find that your character was similar to or different from the one in the screenplay?

I felt that Mia in the screenplay was certainly true to Mia in the Vampire Academy books. Daniel Waters, our brilliant screenwriter, captured Mia's feisty, evil, doll-like personality that was described in the books. The only thing that really differed was my haircut and eye color. In the books, Mia's hair is long and full of blond ringlets, and her eyes are blue. In the film, our director, Mark Waters, allowed me to keep what he called my "signature haircut" and just dyed my hair summer-blond. Additionally, my eyes are brown.

Q: What were some aspects of the film that you felt stood out as unique?

One of the elements I feel is extremely specific to *Vampire Academy* is the presence of not two competing entities, but three. Though most vampires are immortal, the Moroi breed are mortal and are protected from the immortal, evil Strigoi vampires by dhampirs. Further, I think it is rare to find a script in which all the characters are so strong, and the audience will truly

member was so excited to be there, creating a set filled with encouragement and constant excitement. Ed Holcroft made me laugh so much it hurt; Olga is such an incredible actress with an unbelievable sense of humor; Lucy is the sweetest, kindest actress. Zoey is amazing as Rose Hathaway! Everyone in the cast was awesome!

Q: How does fandom come into play when bringing something like this to the screen? Are you ever worried how fans will react?

Of course it's nerve-racking knowing that millions of people have read the books and are counting on us to be the characters they envisioned in their heads. However, as an actor, I try not to worry about what people will think, and focus on just being truthful to who the character is and becoming her to the best of my abilities. After all, if I don't believe I'm Mia, the audience won't either, so I draw all of my concentration to the work and dig as deep as I can to discover who Mia truly is, what scares her, what makes her happy, what her background is, etc. Further, I think every actor brings something special to each

get a sense of the background of each and every character in the film. The characters are incredibly easy to relate to. We all remember the cute guy at school that everyone fought over and wanted to date. We all remember the popular clan of teens who worked tirelessly to cross the bridge from unpopularity to popularity. Everyone who sees the film will be able to recall people from their school that were analogous to the characters in the film, and that is one of the many things that is so great about the story and screenplay.

Q: Were there any other characters that interested you?

Bruno, Mia's close friend, intrigues me. He doesn't say much, but he's always lurking and conspiring with Mia regarding how she will ruin Lissa's life next. I feel like Bruno is the quiet one that no one suspects of anything, but in reality, he's the one behind all of Mia's cleverest showdowns.

Q: What was it like working with the other actors?

Working with the other actors on this film was a phenomenal experience. It was so nice to arrive at work every day and not feel as if I was working at all! Every cast

character that the audience won't expect, but that's what makes the film come to life.

Q: What's your favorite moment in the script?

My favorite moment in the script would be when Mia loses it with Christian, Lissa, and Rose at the dance. Apart from the walls Mia usually puts up to protect herself from being hurt and to mask her lower-class status, Mia really falls apart when she marches into the dance, and we get a sense of how lost she really is. It's easy to sympathize with Mia during this scene, as her vulnerability becomes quite transparent. Although she is the mean girl at school that you'd never want to feel bad for, I know I felt for Mia in this scene. I love that you see who Mia is behind her walls of popularity, and you realize that Mia is extremely insecure and fearful of people seeing her true self.

Q: Were there any surprises you encountered during the shoot?

The only surprise I encountered during shooting was performing all of my own stunts. When reading the script, I guess I assumed the stunts would be minimal, but I actually ended up doing quite a few incredibly cool stunts. On the first two days of filming, we shot the reaction to Rose's punch to Mia, and Mia's subsequent fall. They put mats under me and I'd fall straight onto them after receiving the punch. It was so much fun! I love participating in stunts and ask to do them myself as much as possible, as I believe taking part in such action helps me add another dimension to the character.

Q: What excites you most about this film? Is there anything you can't wait for audiences to see?

The thing that excites me most about this film is the amazing group of collaborators—actors, producers, director, writer—that have all worked so hard to make this film the best it can be. And I'm very excited for audiences to see all of us fang! Every character's fangs are slightly different, and everyone fangs slightly differently, so I can't wait to see the audiences' reactions.

"At first I felt a little bit intimidated when Sami played a scarily convincing Mia, but I quickly learned that Mia and Sami are very different people!"

— LUCY FRY ON SAMI GAYLE AS MIA RINALDI

CAMERON MONAGHAN AS *Mason Ashford*

Mason Ashford just can't catch a break. As a dhampir guardian-in-training, he's driven, focused, and keeps his eye on the prize, though in this case, the prize is fellow novice Rose Hathaway. Mason cares deeply for Rose and he'd do anything he could to be with her. But Rose has eyes for Dimitri, and Mason struggles to accept his role as Rose's best friend, despite his desire for a more romantic relationship. Bringing this character to life is actor Cameron Monaghan, best known for his role as Ian on the Showtime series *Shameless*. Monaghan brings to the part the wide-eyed innocence of youth and a conflicted sensibility that accompanies young, unrequited love. As with the rest of the cast, Monaghan made sure to study up before filming began.

"While I've heard some spoilers from further in the series, I didn't want to read too far ahead, as I wanted my performance to seem present and I thought having knowledge of what happens later on could taint that," he explained. "Mason is the same cheeky bastard he was in the novels. I feel his attitude and persona are very true to the book. With regard to the script, I found the sense of humor very intriguing. It's also a very well-written young adult adaptation, but what differentiated it from other scripts for me was how Dan balanced that aspect with a tongue-in-cheek angle." Monaghan found his character's adoration of Rose Hathaway a key element in his portrayal of Mason Ashford. "I find Mason's unrequited crush on Rose interesting because so much of the time, the 'jilted lover' character tends to come off a bit too self-serving and clueless. I

never got that impression from Mason; he's not petty and selfish. He deeply values his friendship with Rose, and he seems to want to protect her. His romantic feelings bubbling up for her come second, something I respect."

Monaghan's experiences on set were both exciting and frustrating—especially the latter, after injuring himself during the shoot. "My first day was working during the prom scenes," he recalled. "The production was so incredibly elaborate; the lighting, the location, the costumes— everything was jaw-droppingly, gorgeously ornate. I was in awe the entire day," he gushed. "I also broke my hand during the shoot, so that was a bit of a surprise. I filmed a fight scene with Zoey in that condition, and I went straight to a hospital from set for an X-ray to find out it was indeed broken. I had to wear a sling for a while, and there's actually a scene in the movie where you can see my fingers are in a splint."

Despite finding plenty of interesting things about his own character, Monaghan couldn't help but be intrigued by the film's other young hunk, Dimitri. "He's the dark, brooding man of mystery. How could you not be curious about his past?"

Like many of the other *Vampire Academy* actors, Monaghan is keyed into the massive online following that the film has built and is excited for the prospect of finally seeing the fans' reaction. "Oh yes, I have definitely experienced the social media following. They are true fanatics, and I think it's great. There is something really great about having a huge group of people who are so deeply excited about what you are making, and it of course encourages you to make something they'd be proud of. And I'm confident when they sit down in the theater, they'll like what we've created here. It's hard to pick one thing that excites me! Since 'everything' isn't really an acceptable answer, I guess something that excites me is this is a large cast of fresh faces. This is especially true of the talented, undeniably beautiful young actresses, who I believe will have lasting careers, and it's great to see them introduced to the cinema world."

Only time will tell what the future holds for Mason Ashford, but in the meantime, at least the character is in very good hands.

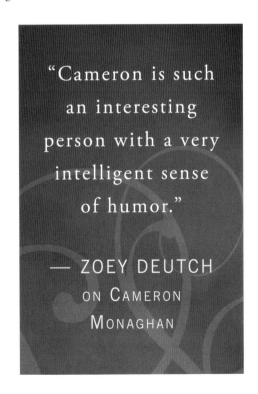

"Cameron is such an interesting person with a very intelligent sense of humor."

— ZOEY DEUTCH
ON CAMERON
MONAGHAN

OLGA KURYLENKO AS *Ellen Kirova*

As Ellen Kirova, the headmistress of St. Vladimir's Academy, actress Olga Kurylenko captures the chillingly cold demeanor that left readers of Richelle Mead's novel a little frosty. She runs the school with an iron fist and won't tolerate any high jinks within its walls, a stark contrast to Kurylenko's sympathetic view of the film's coming-of-age themes.

"*Vampire Academy* is full of punk and rebellion, and it has a great sense of humor," Kurylenko explained. "At the same time, it deals with serious issues about the rites of passage of the young. Fun and adventure sit alongside more profound concerns. It felt more real and truthful than *Twilight*, for example. I thought that it would be great fun to watch, but also I think the subtext and emotional needs of the characters are so strong that audiences will want to connect."

Kurylenko is quick to point out that despite her chilling poise, Kirova is actually a wounded soul who understands far more about her young charges than she allows herself to show. "Kirova is a leader who wants to protect her family, and therefore she can be demanding and

sometimes cold. She is a wise woman who empathizes with the teenagers under her care. We know that what they experience she has also experienced, and that she has been on that same journey. She has been wounded along the way and still carries the scars to prove it. With her there is a strictness and discipline (she can be quite frightening!), but deep down there is real love and kindness in her character. She has everything is takes to be ready for the fight. Expect her to kick some ass!"

As a character, Ellen Kirova may be a looming and threatening presence for the

students at St. Vladimir's, but thankfully the same can't be said for Kurylenko, whose class and professionalism left her young costars in awe.

"It was a surprise to me that Olga was more intimidating than anyone else," confessed Sarah Hyland. "Her beauty literally left me speechless, and I felt like a fourteen-year-old boy every time I was around her."

Kurylenko brings to *Vampire Academy* a collection of accomplishments, having previously appeared in films like *Quantum of Solace* and *Oblivion*, as well as the TV show *Magic City*. Director Mark Waters had nothing but glowing things to say about the French actress.

"I was very pleasantly surprised by Olga Kurylenko, who had never played such a deliciously malevolent character, and who handled huge tracts of dialogue as if she was a practiced Shakespearean thespian."

Kurylenko sums up her experience quite simply. "I arrived to find great sets, great costumes, and great effects. The team was having a real ball with this," she admitted. "They have created a unique world. I don't think readers will be disappointed."

GABRIEL BYRNE AS *Victor Dashkov*
AND JOELY RICHARDSON AS *Queen Tatiana*

Gabriel Byrne boasts an impressive résumé of credits in his thirty-year career: award-winning films like *The Usual Suspects*, box-office smashes such as *Enemy of the State*, plus critically acclaimed television like HBO's *In Treatment*. Intimidating? Perhaps in theory . . . but in practice, the young cast of *Vampire Academy* found themselves taken with Byrne's devotion to his craft and his graciousness as a human being.

"I thought I was going to be intimidated most by Gabriel because he's such an amazing actor that I've looked up to for years," said Sarah Hyland. "But he was so sweet and a very generous scene partner." Hyland's complimentary sentiment was shared with Zoey Deutch.

"Initially, I thought I might be intimidated by Gabriel Byrne, but he was so warm and generous that those feelings dissipated immediately," Deutch echoed. Actress Lucy Fry went even further, describing him as an idol of sorts for his

Mark Waters directs Joely Richardson.

brave and inspiring career choices.

"I also really enjoyed working with Gabriel. No, that's the understatement of the year," Fry corrected. "I was thrilled to work with Gabriel. I deeply admire his work and he is an incredibly intelligent, centered, and peaceful person. We would often talk about where to find quiet nature between a busy film set and the bustle of living in inner-city London. It was such a gift to be able to learn from him about the way he has navigated his career and life choices to stay grounded in this industry."

But Gabriel Byrne wasn't the only respected thespian in the cast. Having come from a famous and successful acting family, Joely Richardson's career accomplishments are

also numerous. She's appeared in more than thirty films and has become well regarded in the industry for her stature and elegance.

"We always want the best actor for the part," explained casting director Marci Liroff. "That said, you have to also put your producer's hat on when we cast. Casting recognizable actors certainly helps. For Queen Tatiana, we needed someone with regal bearing, fiery strength with a side of intensity. That's Joely Richardson! And in terms of Uncle Victor, I wanted someone who exuded strength of character and gentleness at the same time. Byrne's work in the HBO series *In Treatment* was nothing short of brilliant. He can really hold the screen without even uttering a word."

Sarah Hyland, Gabriel Byrne, Zoey Deutch, and Lucy Fry prepare for the next take.

IN HER OWN WORDS: ROISIN CARTY, DIALECT COACH FOR *Vampire Academy*

"My name is Roisin Carty, and I'm the dialect coach for *Vampire Academy*. My job principally involved teaching Lucy Fry to speak with an RP (Standard English) accent, as well as helping Danila Kozlovsky with his first English-speaking role. It was also my job to make sure the various names in the film were pronounced correctly, such as dhampir, Strigoi, and Moroi. Prior to becoming a dialect coach I also taught English as a Foreign Language—so I got a great insight into the challenges facing speakers of English as a second language and how to help them. I originally studied to be a speech therapist but was drawn into the theatrical world very soon after graduating. After completing the voice course at Central School of Speech and Drama, I taught for a couple of years before working on my first film, *Waking Ned*, in 1997. I also worked on the *Lord of the Rings* film trilogy, which I'm quite proud of. It was my second film job, and I was involved from the first day of prep to the recording of the last line of dialogue in ADR for the third film—five years later! From a dialect point of view it was a wonderful project, as it involved not only the teaching of various dialects of English but also bringing to life the languages created by Tolkien. I am also particularly proud of working on the *Hobbit* film trilogy and persuading Peter Jackson that Smaug should be pronounced with the vowel sound in *house* as opposed to the vowel sound in *taught*! One of my all-time favorite films is *Heathers*—so when my agent called me about *Vampire Academy*, I couldn't say no! Also it was a wonderful opportunity to work with Danila and Lucy, as well as meeting Zoey and the rest of the cast. I've

(From left to right) Cameron Monaghan, Sami Gayle, Ashley Charles, Sarah Hyland, Lucy Fry, Richelle Mead, Zoey Deutch, and Dominic Sherwood

been working as a dialect coach in film for sixteen years—in that time I've taught the RP accent to actors from Australia, New Zealand, and the USA as well as to actors from the British Isles. The majority of the Moroi speak with RP accents—for example, Princess Vasilisa and her family, and Christian. The dhampir mostly speak with American accents. There are exceptions to the above, of course, for example: Dimitri (dhampir with a gentle Russian accent) and Spiridon (Northern Irish dhampir). We were very lucky to have an intense two-week rehearsal period during which I worked with both Danila and Lucy as much as four hours a day. They were both very committed to getting their dialects right and worked hard to achieve this. The work was challenging and fun at the same time, and the sessions flew by punctuated by lots of laughter!"

(From left to right) The St. Vladimir's Academy logo; an exterior shot of the Academy itself; an outdoor hallway; and a statue of the mysterious Saint Vladimir

CHAPTER 6

SETTING THE STAGE

RICHELLE MEAD ON THE CREATION OF

St. Vladimir's Academy

"St. Vladimir's Academy serves a lot of different purposes in the series, so I had to consider all of them for its creation. It's not just a school; it's also a sanctuary of sorts. Moroi parents who choose to send their children here are trading family time for safety. Students attend almost year-round and hardly ever see their parents. With those things in mind, I had to put St. Vladimir's in a location that would preserve that high level of safety—both from Strigoi and curious humans. Backwoods Montana—with its vast forests and mountains—became an ideal setting. At the same time, I also had to keep in mind that students like this don't quite have the same experiences that 'normal' students at a private boarding school would have. There's no easy way to get off campus. Field trips are few and far between because safety won't allow it. Once Moroi and dhampirs are there, they pretty much stay there. As such, it was essential to make sure the school was the kind of place where they could live happily. Everything there is the newest and best, despite the façade of historic buildings. Computer labs, athletic facilities, and medicine—all of it is state-of-the-art. Academics are much more extensive than ordinary schools, in the hopes that there's something there for everyone to be interested in. Equally important are the touches of ordinary home life, like religious services, movie lounges, and lots of open green spaces. The message one walks away with is, 'Yes, you do have to spend a lot of time at St. Vladimir's . . . but you'll like it.' If I were a student at St. Vlad's, I'd probably take as many history and literature classes as I could! I love that kind of stuff, and one of the great things about the Moroi is that they have a much greater emphasis on their past and heritage than the rest of us tend to have. This makes a lot more sense when you look at what the Moroi have been through. They've been hunted by the Strigoi and forced to spread out all over the world, sometimes hiding in isolation and sometimes mixing into human cities. When your people live with that kind of danger, preserving your culture becomes imperative. It's the shared heritage that continues to unite the Moroi as a people and allow them to persevere."[16]

ST. VLADIMIR'S ACADEMY

Most schools teach the basics: reading, writing, and arithmetic. But what are students supposed to do if a Strigoi vampire attacks them? You won't learn that kind of defense at just any old high school. At the prestigious St. Vladimir's Academy, however, that type of exercise is just the tip of the iceberg. Named after a mysterious and powerful Russian saint, the Academy is tucked neatly away from prying eyes, deep in the mountains of Montana. In order to protect itself from dangerous Strigoi and any other unwelcome interlopers, the school is guarded by an assortment of magical barriers, as well as an iron fence that spans the large expanse of property. The grounds feature everything a typical boarding school might have: gymnasium, computer lab, library, etc., with one exception, of course. At St. Vladimir's, there's a feeding room near the cafeteria filled with willing humans, where the vampire student body goes for nourishment. The staff is keen to make sure that the human volunteers are well taken care of, and there of their own volition.

The school offers exemplary training for dhampir novices so that they may one day graduate to become full guardians. At St. Vladimir's, they fraternize with Moroi as part of their socialization while attending a variety of classes aimed at making them elite fighting machines. As they enter their junior year, each novice is required to pass a qualifying exam given by a group of visiting superiors in order

Students of St. Vlad's mingle at the Equinox Dance.

The crew prepares to film an exterior shot.

to make it to the next level. If dhampirs are deemed unworthy, they're held at their current level until they pass the qualifier. In extreme cases, they can also be expelled. During their senior year, novices are required to complete six weeks of intense fieldwork that revolves around the constant guardianship of a Moroi ward. During this period of time, the pairing receives a barrage of unexpected assaults aimed at challenging the dhampir's fighting skills as well as protective abilities. If the dhampir's performance is deemed worthy, he or she will graduate and receive a promise mark tattoo. This mark stands as a symbol of that dhampir's unending service as a guardian of the Moroi. There are varying levels of success in the guardian world, and a dhampir that destroys a Strigoi prior to completing training is considered "unpromised" and receives no mark at all. These guardians are seen as lone wolves in the vampire community, unpredictable stalkers who play by their own rules and hunt on their own terms.

MOROI CLASSES: American Colonial Literature, Ancient Poetry, Basics of Elemental Control, Russian, Creative Writing, and Culinary Science

DHAMPIR CLASSES: Advanced Guardian Combat Techniques, Bodyguard Theory, Personal Protection, Weight Training, and Conditioning

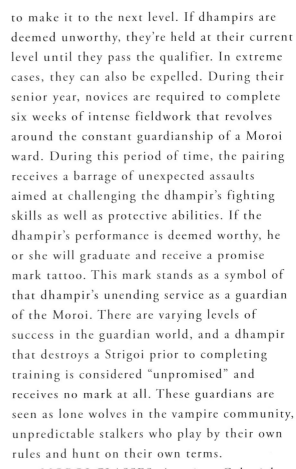

CHARLOTTE WRIGHT, LOCATION MANAGER FOR
Vampire Academy

"My job as a location manager is to work with the director and designer, in the initial stages of production, to pull together the locations that match their vision and style for the film. Once locations are decided on, it is my role to make sure that the shoot runs as smoothly as possible moving from one location to the next, and to deliver all the director's requests, whether it be lighting, camera, design, stunts, etc., at each location; so there is always a stage of intense negotiations with the locations prior to the shooting crew arriving to start filming the scenes. The first step in my process is always to read the script, which will give me my own vision of the film before being briefed by both director and designer on their vision and style. In this instance, I did not read the book first due to the time frame of preproduction for myself, but would always read the book as well, ideally. It is usually the designer who has the style in his head he would like to sell to the director. My job is to try and keep up and match their vision with reality. My job requires some creative thinking, but it's absolutely essential to spend time, in the very early stages of preproduction, driving the director and designer to different location options to allow them to start to picture their vision in reality on location. As there was a lot of night filming, I felt that the exterior locations had to offer interesting architecture and shapes so that with the night backdrop there was scale, shape, and interest rather than flat landscapes or flat buildings. This then created the grand, slightly mysterious, and

sometimes 'dark' setting to the scenes. Both the opening scenes read as being very punchy and dramatic . . . action-packed. Also, the final fight scenes and escape scenes from the Dashkovs' lodge were going to be challenging and exciting.

"The film is also set in America, so trying to film in England and make the film look as if we were in the States was going to be a challenge—which I hope has worked well. We shot in approximately fifteen locations in total; mainly in London or the surrounding counties. There are always risks and unknowns when choosing locations. There was only one really main problem throughout the film that sent the locations team into a spin. We had been carefully negotiating with a location that was giving us a controlled street environment where we were able to shoot our opening scene of the film, which included a stunt explosion. The street was multi-tenanted, and a few weeks before filming, scaffolding went up outside one of the hero buildings in the shot and was not going to be coming down again before our shoot dates. Having to deliver this sort of news was always difficult, as you never want to be in the unenviable position of asking the director to adjust his vision at such a late stage while he is also mid-shoot. A solution was found, though, and we plowed ahead, with the end result looking great. Director Mark Waters was fantastic. He was very direct and always made time for me if needed. He also knew very clearly what he liked and what he did not like, and we seemed to move through things fairly swiftly. I think the kids will love the concept of the film and engage in it. I can't wait for the great locations used to be on-screen in the States, as there were some fantastic period film locations used; so I hope it's a showcase of what the UK can offer."

The crew sets the ominous mood by backlighting the statue of St. Vladimir.

IN HER OWN WORDS: LISA CHUGG
Set Decorator

"My name is Lisa Chugg, and I am the set decorator on *Vampire Academy*. I worked closely with the production designer and director to dress the constructed sets and locations so that they are ready to shoot. My job involved heading a team that sources every prop for the film, from the wallpaper and carpet to the tables and chairs and cutlery, to the food the actors eat on-screen! Everything but the constructed set. I've worked with Frank Walsh, the production designer, on a number of films, including *Inception*, *Hereafter*, and *Agora*, so Frank approached me to work with him again on this project. Part of my job is to be able to focus on any period in time and produce great-looking sets. *Inception* and *Agora* were films that range over two thousand years apart in time—but both very challenging for very different reasons. One of my favorite parts of my job is research. One day I'll be learning how to dress an eel-smoking cabinet, and the next, walking around huge airplane scrapyards looking for cockpit dials! No two days are the same, and I get to see some very interesting places. With *Vampire Academy*, my first step was to read the script and break it down into the different sets required. I then did lots of research, and through talking and looking at this research with the designer, we refined a 'look' for the sets: everything from color palettes and style of furniture to what personal belongings the characters might possess. I then met with the director and got feedback and thoughts on my ideas. I also worked closely with the director of photography and lighting department to

make sure practical lighting worked and had the right mood. I also liaised with the costume designer to make sure the colors in our sets didn't clash with our lead actors' costumes!

"Mark and I had quite a few meetings in preproduction where I showed him mood boards I had put together of every set, and my thoughts for how the sets should look; these boards comprise fabric swatches, furniture ideas, wallpaper samples, color palettes, etc. This is a very important part of the process where I get to know what Mark is thinking, and he tells me if there are important elements he wanted to include that were not necessarily scripted. Generally, we agreed on most things. Mark was great to work with in that he had a very clear vision of what he wanted from the start—which was really helpful for me. If there was something Mark wanted to change, there was generally a reason; for example, the action required a sofa instead of a chair, or a curtain to be drawn rather than a blind pulled down, etc. The set decoration office walls are usually renowned for being covered floor to ceiling with prop photos, reference images, and fabric swatches. We surround ourselves with images! On this project, I had references ranging from old headmistresses' offices in the 1940s to ultra-modern spas. I also looked at photographer Lise Sarfati's work. Inspiration can come from one tiny image in a book or an image found online. A big challenge on *Vampire Academy* was that the main unit did a lot of night shoots—so it was sometimes difficult to get time to speak with the crew regarding pre-dressing requirements to make sure they had what they needed. Surprises usually came from location restrictions—where something you intended to do was suddenly not possible.

However, thinking our way out of problems can sometimes lead to a more interesting look . . . so it's not always a bad thing! I thought *Vampire Academy* was a great script, and the look of the film is unusual in that it mixes tradition with modernity—and this makes the sets unique."

Zoey Deutch and Dominic Sherwood listen intently as Mark Waters gives direction for the forthcoming scene.

"The book and the script are so well written. I knew it was just about keeping up the search until we found exactly the right person for each part. There should be no settling."

—MARCI LIROFF

CHAPTER 7
DRESS CODE

THE CAST SYSTEM:
MARCI LIROFF TALKS ABOUT
Finding the Right Actors

Contrary to popular belief, actors do not magically appear on film sets when the time comes to make a movie. They're chosen carefully from a select group of professional actors whose unique talents are right for a project. This process is spearheaded by one of the most essential roles in the entertainment industry, a role that can often be overlooked by the average filmgoer: the casting director. This title seems fairly straightforward from the outside, but a casting director's function is actually layered. Once a film project has been set into motion, a casting director sits down with the movie's director to discuss ideas and break down character types. Then comes research and numerous levels of auditions before the director and creative team finally decide which actors are best suited for the roles. A casting director is often called upon during these final rounds to offer a fresh perspective when it comes to an actor's potential. Many times actors may not necessarily fit the basic breakdown criteria. They may be slightly shorter or of a different ethnic background than the character for which they audition. Casting directors look beyond those minuscule differences for the spark in a performer that transcends simple classification. They look for potential that can be molded and shaped into

Mason Ashford (Cameron Monaghan) confides in Rose Hathaway

something new and exciting. It's a difficult role to be sure, but it's also an incredibly important one. Marci Liroff is an industry veteran with a legendary résumé: *Indiana Jones and the Temple of Doom*, *E.T.*, and *Poltergeist* are just some of the memorable and groundbreaking films she's had a hand in shaping over the past twenty-five years. So when an old friend approached her to cast *Vampire Academy*, it was a no-brainer for an accomplished authority like Liroff.

"Mark Waters and I have collaborated on all of his films from *Freaky Friday* until *Vampire Academy*. We have sort of a shorthand at this point," explained Liroff. "I know his taste, and he trusts mine. We like the healthy debate, and I know when to push back and stand up for my casting choices. I love working with him because he's very knowledgeable

about so many actors out there and is open to discovering new ones."

The mythological world of Moroi, Strigoi, and dhampirs can be overwhelming for the uninitiated, but Liroff was soon taken with the world of *Vampire Academy* after a quick read of Daniel Waters's screenplay. "Quite honestly, this genre is not my thing," she confessed. "That said, once I read the screenplay, I was a convert. I was hooked! This story and screenplay belie the genre. They turn it on its head. Once I read the script, I knew I had some great characters to sink my teeth into and was inspired to find the right actors . . . pun intended!"

The Vampire Academy book series has laid out a large and diverse cast of characters and an in-depth mythology. By any standard, there are a myriad of

Sonya Karp, played by Claire Foy

Mark Waters and Joely Richardson (Queen Tatiana)

expectations to juggle in bringing Richelle Mead's vision to the screen and appeasing the growing, rabid fan base. Liroff kept herself on track by focusing her attention squarely on Daniel Waters's adaptation. "When I started the project, I wanted to be true to the screenplay and not reference the books. I wanted to be sure that I was getting *all* my information from the script—and not peripherally from my knowledge of the books. In contrast, my casting associate Michelle Levy *inhaled* all of the books in a few weeks, so along with the writer Dan Waters, and our director Mark Waters, she was my go-to person for all things *Vampire Academy*."

But the allure of Mead's complex characters quickly brought her into the fold, and soon Liroff was taken with the book's emotional mythos. "About halfway through the casting process I finally broke down and couldn't resist cracking the first book. I couldn't put it down. In the end, it actually helped me cast these characters because I also had an understanding of the fans' expectations, which is an important factor here. I am now a true fan of the book series."

Once she'd gotten a feel for the world of *Vampire Academy*, the real work began: the search for the perfect cast. But each new project presents its own set of challenges. Finding a simple, basic type in an industry full of willing and hungry

Lissa Dragomir is ready for action.

actors might seem easy, but the truth of the matter is slightly more complex. In the case of the Academy's brawny Russian bruiser, Liroff found herself in a bit of a pickle. "The most challenging role was Dimitri," she admitted. "As you know, he's written as a six-foot-seven Russian 'god,' for lack of another word! Not a lot of actors who fit that description are walking around Hollywood. I knew I had to find someone who was very tall, extremely charismatic, and Russian . . . but for me I'm always looking for the strongest actor for the part." A casting director's quest can lead in a variety of directions, but thankfully modern technology has been able to bring actors to the forefront who might not have had a chance at face time in the past. "I did a worldwide search for this character, and we interviewed hundreds of guys in person and online

Natalie and Lissa take shade from the sun.

through their self-submitted auditions and on Skype. God bless the Internet!"

The casting process can be a grueling one for both the creative team and the actors. As modern films delve deeper into the human condition and characters become increasingly layered, it can be challenging to find actors that capture the eccentricities and nuances of the roles for which they audition. At the heart of the Vampire Academy world is the complicated relationship between Rose Hathaway and Lissa Dragomir. Casting these two characters required careful consideration of not just an actor's look and demeanor, but also the potential for something more.

"In our very first concept meeting, Mark brought up Zoey as Rose and said we could do a 'Linda Hamilton' on her . . . meaning she could train like Hamilton did for *Terminator 2*. I knew of Zoey because her parents and I know each other. I cast her father Howie Deutch's first movie, *Pretty in Pink*. I cast her mother, Lea Thompson, in one of her first films, *All*

Olga Kurylenko as the stern Kirova

the Right Moves, with Tom Cruise. Once Zoey came in, I just knew she was the one. She had it all going on. Zoey brings her own brand of sass and strength—and her comedy timing makes her stand out. She definitely has the 'don't mess with me' thing down! Her timing is never forced . . . she knows exactly where to land

The bond between Zoey Deutch and Danila Kozlovsky extends beyond the characters they play in *Vampire Academy*.

a line. Her beauty is unique, and I think she's got such great screen presence. She's going to be a big star from this film."

After finding the perfect Rose, Liroff and Waters turned their attention toward casting the young Miss Hathaway's ward and best friend, Lissa Dragomir. Though the search proved difficult, they were soon taken with actress Lucy Fry's ability to convey Lissa's tentative and delicate nature while retaining the character's sovereign sensibility.

"Casting Lissa was a bit more of a challenge," Liroff revealed. "We were about to do our screen tests for Lissa and Rose when I received a self-submitted tape from Lucy Fry from Australia. It turned out she had gotten to L.A. just a few days earlier. When we put her together with Zoey, she had the regal bearing of a princess as well as a childlike quality of vulnerability that needed protecting. For an actress with not a lot of experience under her belt, she had an uncanny sense of how to inhabit this character. Lucy is a very smart and sensitive girl. There's something about her that makes you want to protect her at all times."

When shooting finally commenced, Liroff experienced firsthand the power of *Vampire Academy*'s passionate fan base. "I've spent some time with Lucy, Zoey, and Danila, and posted photos on Instagram," she recalled. "People went crazy, and now I see them popping up all over the Internet. I've been very involved in social media for the last several years, though I've not been involved on a project with such a huge fan base as this. The fan base is so amazing, considering the film hasn't even been released yet! I check into the Facebook fan page from time to time to see what they're talking about, and people tweet to me all the time about the film."

Years of hard work and creative triumphs can bring about a great deal of insight, but Liroff keeps her storied body of work in perspective. She's cast numerous iconic films over the last thirty years, but her philosophy is a simple one and it starts in her own home. "Putting together a great cast is like putting together the perfect dinner party. You have to have the right people at the table *and* you have to have the right people sitting next to each other," she explained. "I throw *very* good dinner parties!"

NAME: Marci Liroff
CAREER HIGHLIGHTS: *E.T. the Extra-Terrestrial, A Christmas Story, St. Elmo's Fire, Mean Girls*
HOW SHE GOT HER START: "I worked as an assistant at ICM for about a year and a half. From there, I heard about a casting job and started working at Fenton-Feinberg Casting for about five years and cast many films there. After seeing *E.T.*, the producers of *Footloose* ran into Steven Spielberg and asked him who cast it—he told them about me and they offered me the film to cast. I brought it into the company and left shortly thereafter to start my own business."
WHAT KEEPS HER COMING BACK FOR MORE: "Working with filmmakers to help them bring their words and vision to life is very exciting to me. Putting together the perfect ensemble of actors is an art form in and of itself and it's what makes me tick."

Victor Dashkov (Gabriel Byrne) admires his fangs.

VAMPIRE ACADEMY: BLOOD SISTERS

SLATE   TAKE

6   1   G
                 T

DIR: MARK WATERS
DOP: TONY PIERCE-ROBERTS BSC

While the majority of the casting process happened in the States, when the production moved to the United Kingdom, casting director Reg Poerscout-Edgerton was brought on board to aid in the search for local actors to flesh out a handful of remaining cast members, including the integral role of Christian Ozera.

"To be honest, when I got into casting it wasn't a career I was really aware of, let alone seeking; it was a happy accident that I wound up in this profession. I came to London for university fifteen years ago to study electronical engineering, completed my first year early, and needed to earn some money. So at the age of nineteen, I got a job as the casting runner on *Band of Brothers*, and it went from there. That was a perfect introduction to the industry, working on a first-class production and getting to meet Tom Hanks (who produced it), as well as many great young actors, some of whom have gone on to have incredible careers. As an assistant/ associate, I worked for some of the top casting directors in the UK and just six years ago was lucky enough to be given my first job as a casting director when Guy Ritchie asked me to cast *RocknRolla*. In the relatively short time I've been a casting director, I've worked with some of the most respected directors in the world on some incredible projects. I have to admit that I didn't know anything about the Vampire Academy books at first. Though obviously I'm a big fan now! Richelle has written some wonderful characters in this series, and it's a joy for a casting director. I couldn't wait to meet Mark to talk about it. He'd been working on the film for a while and had already cast the main characters with Marci Liroff. There's such a strong fan base for the books; there's also a concern of whether how you picture the characters is how the fans have pictured them. With Christian, we read the scene where he first meets Lissa, and we also read scenes between him and Rose—where obviously they have very different dynamics. From the first time Dominic Sherwood came in, he just had 'it.' I work very much on instinct and he just felt right to me (and luckily, Mark agreed!). He's got the looks and charm of a film star, but also a certain vulnerability that, despite all his obvious attributes, makes you believe he could be a tortured soul who's endured the pain of losing his parents and been suffering the rejection of his peers. He also does the perfect Christian Ozera sardonic smirk . . ."

RUTH MYERS:
Costume Designer

"After meeting with the director and discussing his ideas, I spent a lot of time thinking, drawing, and making color charts. Mark Waters had strong visual ideas that I found easy to relate to. He's an excellent and totally prepared director with a very clear sense of what he is looking for, which made my job a lot more exciting and gave me room to expand his vision. He had a very firm idea of color palette, which I loved. I wanted to design the film with great style, but also with the vitality of youth. We put the students into uniforms, which, although not in the book, I hope gave the film a strong sense of place and time and accentuated their youth. I responded to the script's freshness and quirkiness from the first reading and felt that it is a very different way of looking at the world of vampires."—**Ruth Myers, costume designer**

A typical uniform worn by students at St. Vladimir's Academy.

"I'm obsessed with Ruth Myers, the costume designer, and the school uniform she made me. The minute I put on my leather jacket, I felt like Rose."

— ZOEY DEUTCH ON COSTUME DESIGNER RUTH MYERS

105

The dress Lissa wore to the Equinox Dance

Concept Artist

"My role involves generating ideas and designs in visual form, to suit the needs of the script. As concept artists on *Vampire Academy*, we worked very closely with the production designer, who briefed us on each task to be completed. This involved us generating ideas for props, environment designs, and sometimes costume elements. For prop design, the initial process was generating a lot of different options for the director to consider, and once a decision was made, we took that idea and refined it to ensure it was feasible before it was constructed. For environments, there may have been an existing location that needed to be embellished. We again worked closely with the production designer to produce visuals that conveyed the right information based on scale, mood, materials, lighting, and so forth. As concept artists, by nature, we will all have our own spin on a given idea. As professionals, we have to keep in mind that our role is to work within the confines of the script, and to produce what is appropriate and fits the director's vision. Much of the communication with the director is done via our production designer, who in turn guides us in the right direction. The director on *Vampire Academy* was very open with his feedback when he came to see what we were producing, which was great. I think elements such as the feeder rooms gave a heightened sense of reality; the environments were totally tangible, which added weight to the more fantastical activities happening within. I was pleased to be working on key objects such as the vampire stakes, taking them from the practice version for learning, through to the final fighting weapons seen in the film. It is satisfying to create something that features in the character's journey. The stake weapons were quite striking; the clean lines and finish work effectively in the high-octane fight scenes. Inspiration often comes from something related to the task at hand; for example, when working on jewelry elements, we would look to various period pieces for inspiration on detailing and decoration. It is important to draw on what has gone before when creating something new. I think as a whole, it's very exciting to have readers of the books and new fans alike see these adventures in motion and on the big screen. I'm sure it will prove to be a hit."

The gold-and-diamond rose pendant that Rose desires from their trip to the mall.

Stunt coordinator Jimmy O'Dee counsels Zoey Deutch on how to maneuver for the next scene.

"I realized the day before that I had to shoot all of my fighting and stunt work with four- to five-inch heels on in a tight prom dress—that was a pretty big curveball to me— while wearing colored contacts, which really impaired my vision. It was hard, but I was up for the challenge and ended up taking great pride in wearing the heels for all three days."

— SARAH HYLAND ON HER STUNT WORK IN
VAMPIRE ACADEMY

CHAPTER 8
BUILDING THE CURRICULUM

Q&A WITH STUNT COORDINATOR JIMMY O'DEE

Q: Describe for us what your role as stunt coordinator entailed on the *Vampire Academy* film.

My job was to devise, design, invent, and then arrange the safe execution of all action on the film, including fights. It is also my job to work closely with the director on the themes and styles of the action. I then have to manage and schedule my department, including budgeting and administration of the department. I have to write risk assessments and method statements and comply with health and safety legislation. I also employ suitable stunt performers who can carry out the action safely and deliver a good performance. I will then previz (previsualize) the fights and action and show Mark to get his feedback on it, to see if he likes it or if he wants to change anything. Then, when he's happy, I'll get the previz (previsualization) off to the various departments that might be interested in seeing it for planning purposes (i.e., props, SFX, camera, construction, set decoration, etc.). The producers are also keen to see what the action is going to look like, so they get a copy.

Danila Kozlovsky makes sure his harness is secured before his stunt.

Q: How did you end up working on the film?

I got a call from the production manager, Eve Swannell, whom I had just worked with on *Kick-Ass 2*. The director, Mark Waters, was keen to meet me for various reasons. I met him in a hotel in London, and we instantly hit it off. I had some ideas about a style of vampire fighting, which would be based on aikido, and Mark had studied aikido when he was younger and was keen for this style to be a base form for the guardians. He invited me on board straightaway. I was actually due to start another film, which would

have meant I wouldn't have been able to do *Vampire Academy*, but luckily for me, that film was pushed, so it all worked out. During that meeting, Mark and I were talking about a theme and a style that would translate and carry through the book series. He was definitely not looking at this as a one-off film. He was keen that whatever I came up with in terms of fight style . . . that it should resonate through the books to show a steady progression of the characters' development. The producers were also very supportive and felt the same.

Q: What are some previous experiences that helped you prepare for the *Vampire Academy* shoot?

I have been in the stunt business for twenty-two years, so I have a lot of film and stunt experience. My personal experience that I think helped with the show is I've been a martial artist since I was eight years old, and I hold a fifth-degree black belt in aikido; I have an additional four black belts in various weapon arts and I also used to work as an instructor for bodyguard courses. This was specifically useful when devising techniques for fighting the Strigoi. They are very strong, badass vampires who are just out to kill, so I came up with a system of fighting that uses bodyguard and aikido techniques. I'm also a vampire genre fan and have seen virtually every vampire series there has been. I was keen to do something different and think that I've done that. This feels fresh and very now and practical.

Q: What were some of the fights and stunts you were a part of for the *Vampire Academy* shoot?

I was behind all of the stunts and fight scenes. With Mike Lambert, I came up with a system that takes a guardian

from a total beginner to an expert: with a stake; without a stake; disarm techniques; multiple attack; two, three, and four against one, both defense and attack. I called them the moon patterns; grade ranges are White Moon, Blue Moon, Red Moon, and Black Moon. And within each level you have one quarter, one half, New Moon, and Full Moon. Then you get into "Blood Master" levels, with Blood Master Level 7 the highest level (at the moment). Dimitri is Blood Master 7. We have our own St. Vladimir's salute. I've developed a subtlety and philosophy in technique, e.g., hiding your fang and showing your fang, symbolized by the stake. It's pretty cool. I had a lot of fun coming up with these. It's an actual system that works; if you were to learn it, you would be a competent fighter!

Q: What risks were involved in the fight sequences and how did they differ from previous experiences?

All fight scenes have risks attached, but if you can train the actors with the proper timing and manage it carefully in sections, you can up the intensity gradually and build the right mind-set and confidence required. I have a great stunt team, and they are all safety-conscious and responsible professionals, so I know they will be as safe as can be, particularly when working with the actors. I used stunt doubles for the trickier, more dangerous bits.

Q: Were there any surprises you encountered during shooting?

I was and wasn't surprised about the level of dedication the actors had toward their training and action sequences. They all threw themselves into it 120 percent. Zoey arrived from the States tired, I think, and then was faced with me and my team saying "Right, young lady; eat this, train here, do this, do that, faster, higher, better—now stretch," and I think she was like, "Oh my God, what have I got myself into?" But with my hand on my heart, she knocked it for six, she trained hard, and even if she didn't want to, she gave it her

all; and I was like a proud big brother when she did her scenes. That attitude didn't change throughout the hectic shoot schedule, and she was really professional in her approach to her training. It really matters to her that Rose Hathaway is as badass as she can be. She knows what these books mean to fans and doesn't want to cheat anybody. She was a joy, and that was my surprise. I have to add that Danila was another one; he was a machine and trained like a world-class athlete to get into shape for his role. We had to bulk him up and teach him around twenty-five fight routines, and he just sucked it up and took it all in. He's a lovely man and an absolutely dedicated actor. He reminded me of Christian Bale, whom I worked with on Batman. He's another one that is totally dedicated to whatever his role may be.

Q: What was it like working with the actors? Were they able to pick up the moves quickly? What were the challenges?

As I said previously, Zoey, Danila, Ben Peel, Sarah Hyland, Cameron, Ryan, Dominique, and all the cast threw themselves into the training with real zeal and dedication. They all got the basic guardian and stake training, including moon patterns, and then they had their individual fights taught to them using the moon patterns and St. Vladimir's fighting style as a base. It worked really well. They all picked up the moves so well that they did more than 90 percent of their fights, which gives more flexibility with the camera, as you don't have to hide doubles, etc. The biggest challenge for my team was the time I had with the actors. It was a tight schedule, and so we had to be very disciplined about when we trained the actors and make sure that they were ready to do their scenes when we turned on the cameras. Sometimes it was tight, but we got through it.

Q: Was there anything from the book series that you were excited to translate for the screen?

I was keen to keep it close to the books but also give the fans my interpretation of the guardians' training and fight style, which isn't obvious from just reading the books. In this sense, you have carte blanche to develop an entire fight philosophy. I think we got the balance right. And it was fun to do.

The main characters had very clear roles, and Dimitri is, of course, godlike— and had to act like it. He was to be responsible, confident, skilled, and very serious, which Danila does brilliantly; but in real life, he's such a comedian and always joking around. I think Mark has got the tone bang on; he knows the books backward,

as does Dan. On set, Mark would often say things like, "In book three, such and such happens and we're doing this, and in book five, we're doing that . . . can this be done, or how would I make this effect?" and so on, so Mark is keen to be true to the books, but add a slant or viewpoint that isn't clearly set out in the books. It's exciting, as he is such a fan and wants to make a film he wants to see. Mark, Dan, and I were chatting just before wrap, close to the end of the shoot, and they were explaining that there isn't as much action in book two, but there is a huge backstory that they could explain as the book played out—they could run a separate thread full of action explaining the backstory regarding Strigoi, etc. They are keen to make an exciting series, and I believe they are doing just that. It's great to be a part of.

Q: Is there anything you can't wait for audiences to see?

The fights and training are pretty cool. There's one fight where Dominique and Danila fight twelve guards, and then Danila and Ben Peel, who plays Spiridon, have a real gritty hand-to-hand fight, which looked great, and so I'm keen for audiences to see that.

Q: What previous credits are you particularly proud of?

I'm proud of most of my past credits, but I guess *Kick-Ass* and *Kick-Ass 2* are the most current, and they were a lot of fun to make, and very good movies. *Rush* is going to be a great movie, so I'm looking forward very much to seeing that, as is *Gravity*, which was a groundbreaking CGI technological experiment with Sandra Bullock and George Clooney. Both are incredibly good actors, so I'm looking forward to that, as we did things that have not been done before.

Storyboard Artist

"My name is John Greaves, and I am the storyboard artist on the production. This job involves putting into a visual form how the film will be shot. This is how I approach creating the storyboards: First, I familiarize myself fully with the script. I then meet with the director to talk through various sequences. I find it best to write myself a shot list. From this, I draw a simple thumbnail board that I can discuss with the director. He will then usually make some adjustments, and then once he's happy with it, I will draw up a finished board, which will be distributed to the crew so that everyone has an idea how the scene will be shot and what will be required for it. It's hard nowadays to find something that is completely unique, but certainly the Strigoi were interesting and fun to draw. I enjoyed the big fight at the end. With storyboards, it's important to get as much information down as quickly and economically as possible, so one doesn't really have time for battles. If it looks okay, it'll do. It's about information, not pretty pictures, unfortunately. Mark and I met on a regular basis to discuss the boards and how they were developing. I got on very well with him and found him extremely easy to work with. My goal on the film was to try to create a storyboard that was both informative and entertaining for the crew. I hope that I achieved that. I'm sure that the film will be a huge success, though I suspect I'm a little outside the target audience . . . by several years."

"My goal on the film was to try to create a storyboard, that was both informative and entertaining for the crew. I hope that I achieved that. I'm sure that the film will be a huge success, though I suspect I'm a little outside the target audience . . . by several years."

— JOHN GREAVES

IN HIS OWN WORDS: MARC JOUVENEAU
Vfx Supervisor

"It's my job to lead the Prime Focus World visual effects team in our collaboration with the director, Mark Waters, to deliver all the VFX for *Vampire Academy*. This project was an exciting and ambitious one. Our first step was to work with Mark and the rest of the creative team to find all the ways in which we could subtly support and enhance the storytelling—being careful not to take over. It was essential to keep the focus on our heroines and the fascinating world they inhabit: a mixture between our world and one full of magic, mystery, vampires, and demonic hounds! Far and away, the challenge that I most looked forward to in bringing the book to life was a chance to realize the psi-hounds! They obviously stand out as unique creatures, but for

all of the magic and fantastical elements we brought to the picture, whether it was the manipulation of fire and water or the bond between Rose and Lissa, we endeavored to imbue them all with that unique quality that can only exist in the world we're helping to create. On a lot of projects, there's an element of trial and error (and sometimes debate) as we work toward a coherent vision, but Mark and his team aren't new to working with VFX and were great collaborators for us. Honestly, there was nothing that had to be fought for; it sounds soppy, but we were all working together from day one to make the best film possible. The struggle is always time! As soon as the camera starts rolling on the first day of shooting we can feel the clock ticking! The race is on from then right up until the premiere to deliver an exciting, beautiful, scary, and (most importantly) fun movie! Mark's vision for this movie was very precise, which is always a pleasure to work with. Every shot in his movie has a role to play in telling the story, and as soon as you understand what that purpose is, it becomes a lot easier to help him get that vision on the screen. We generated a lot of our own art while developing the look of the psi-hounds; our jumping-off point was a lot of real reference of wolves and dogs (and crossbred wolf dogs!). Watching footage of how they move and act also really helped us to make the most of every shot they have on screen. I can't wait to see the entire movie! I'm not going to give anything away, but aside from the hounds, I'm especially excited to see those final shots . . ."

PSI-HOUNDS

The psi-hounds are hulking, wolf-like creatures that share a psychic connection with their Moroi masters. The enchanted beasts travel in roving packs, and their eyes have a fiery orange glow.

"At first we thought we could train actual dogs to be our psi-hounds. We soon realized that no matter how much we worked with them, they would always be happily wagging their tails and tongues and would never look menacing. That's why we ended up creating CGI hounds who, I think, look much more like Richelle originally envisioned them, and who are definitely much more scary than our sweet trained dogs."
—Director Mark Waters on the psi-hounds

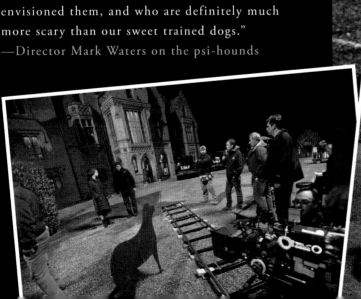

"I was pleasantly surprised by how close I became with Mark Waters. By the end of the movie he felt like family, and it was really wonderful knowing he had my back."

—ZOEY DEUTCH ON MARK WATERS

CHAPTER 9
CLASS IN SESSION

MARK WATERS
Director

There are an incredible amount of romantic notions that surround the world of filmmaking, and the director's role often holds a particular fascination with moviegoers. Images from the classic days of Hollywood would have everyone believing that the director shows up on set with a bullhorn, shouting commands and storming around until his demands are met. While this image is certainly entertaining, it isn't all that truthful. The reality is that it takes more than a few experienced professionals to make a movie, but the one at the helm of it all is the director. A director's job is to see the big picture. He or she must be aware, and concerned about all aspects of film production, whether it's the lighting for a simple exterior shot, the blocking for an elaborate fight scene, or the way an actor's costume fits. The director has to be able to see and solve a problem before anyone ever knows about it, at least in theory. A director must mold, meld, and shape a production so that the story it presents is seamless. During the process, ideas are shared, changed, and often trashed. But ultimately, once a vision is laid out, it must be executed. The person that is in charge of making that happen is—you guessed it—the director.

Mark Waters gets a different perspective on setting up the next shot.

Mark Waters utilizes modern technology to get a different perspective on a scene.

Mark Waters has an impressive and varied résumé. From indie darling *The House of Yes* to the mainstream hit *Mean Girls*, Waters has had a hand in crafting stories for a diverse list of characters. In Richelle Mead's *Vampire Academy*, Waters saw the chance to bring to the screen a realistic depiction of young adult life that just happens to take place at a vampire boarding school. Though filled with occult subject matter, the core of Mead's fable is rooted in the relationship between Rose Hathaway and Lissa Dragomir. In their bond, Waters saw something authentic and worth exploring on film.

"I connected to having a heroine like Rose, who was decidedly brash and imperfect, who caused as many problems as she solved, and who was just as likely to say the wrong thing as the right thing.

The book's entire tone, the veer from deadly serious to hilariously sarcastic, is exactly the sensibility that I relate to. If two guys have a conflict with each other, they have the straightforward and crude outlet of simply punching each other until their conflict is miraculously resolved. This is not really available to young women in high school, so the ways they compete and resolve conflicts is inevitably more interesting, funny, and frightening to watch."

Movies that handle fantasy elements like vampires and magic are often clumped together by the viewing public as merely genre films, but Waters is quick to point out that *Vampire Academy* stands apart from the pack because of its unique humor and honest sensibility. "*Twilight* was about a naive person who knew nothing of a certain world, basically discovering that this world existed and totally being indoctrinated into it and falling in love with a vampire, which is interesting," Waters explained. "It's also different from *Harry Potter* in that sense. This is about two people who are deeply embedded in this world, and the audience is the one who is taking the journey of being transported and learning about it for the first time, while the characters are deeply, deeply in it and trying to just live and survive day to day. I find a lot of YA movies . . . are almost kind of navel-gazing in a sense of sincerity and self-importance. I think the nature of this material is that it doesn't go that direction. Even when things are deadly serious, they are still really kept interesting and kept in a place where we never lose that wit and humor, which is kind of the thing that my brother and I like to do in all movies. I think the big difference, tonally, from the other movies that you could say are kind of globally put under the YA genre, really comes from that humor and subversive wit that comes from my brother's writing and from Richelle Mead's book themselves. I think every person who reads the book has their own images that come to mind when they read it, just like I do, and part of my job is . . . I read things and imagine them and then start trying to take what I imagine and make it visual for everybody else to see. It just happens to be my personal vision, and every person's is going to be different— every book reader. As soon as I signed on to the project, my brother and I flew up to

Mark Waters casts his own playful spell on Lucy Fry during some downtime between takes.

Seattle and sat down with Richelle Mead and talked about all the books. The good news is that she loved the screenplay and thought it was hilarious and thought it very much captured her books while still kind of adding, making things more cinematic and putting the action on steroids—but never straying too far from being loyal to her story lines and loyal to her characters. It just so happens in this movie that the stakes and the drama and the intensity of it are real in the sense that, yes, they're going through classic things about 'Does this boy like me or not,' 'Is this girl out to get me,' but at the same time underplaying all of this is a true life-and-death saga because they are vampires who have predatory, evil vampires out to kill them. It makes everything very potent because . . . there actually are real, scary stakes and an urgency going on at all times."[17]

Fans will also be delighted to know that most all of their favorite elements from Mead's book were given time to shine in the final product. "Oddly, not much had to be cut from the book, perhaps just accelerated.

As far as things that only existed in the script, the moment that really tickles me is when Lissa succumbs to giving the first high five of her life to Rose."

With so many components to consider, Waters and his team worked overtime to make sure that everyone understood the needs of the shoot. "Because we didn't have a lot of time to shoot several elaborate action sequences, everything had to be really mapped out. I like to work with old-school storyboard artists and draw and redraw the shots until we know the shots and cuts we're going to need. Then we have several meetings with all tech department heads where we figure out how we are going to actually shoot all the things we envisioned. I also realized that it's very difficult to shoot a vampire movie at a location that's above a latitude of fifty degrees north—like London, where we shot—because you only get about six hours of night, so you need to be very tricky and efficient to shoot without your Moroi getting a bad sunburn."

Waters insists he never played favorites with actors and that "everyone was strong and everyone exceeded expectations" but admits, at least cosmetically, that a couple of cast members

"During the shoot, my brother provided me with many mixtapes that were comically on theme with the movie, with songs ranging from 'Bela Lugosi's Dead' (by Bauhaus) to 'My Blood' by Ellie Goulding to 'If You Want Blood' by AC/DC."
— DIRECTOR MARK WATERS

fit his mental image perfectly. "The two characters/actors who look the most like the way I envisioned them from the book were Cameron Monaghan as Mason and Ashley Charles as Jesse. In the shooting process, they both ended up transcending my imagination of their characters."

With filming complete, Waters and his team are anxious to see if their interpretation of Mead's story gives audiences a brand-new angle to consider in their coming-of-age vampire tale. The director is quick to point out that his addition to the Vampire Academy mythos "remains to be seen and will be determined by the fans," but if current buzz is any indication, this could be the first of many trips back to the world of St. Vladimir's for Waters and his stellar crew of industry professionals.

"Our director, Mark Waters, was a dream to work with and allowed me to try every scene a myriad of different ways so that, by the end of the day, I felt as if I had exerted every path I could have taken in every scene and had the sky as my limit. The producers felt like family . . .

Daniel Waters, the screenplay writer, became a huge film mentor to me . . . I really hope the happiness and love on the set translates to the screen. Moreover, I'm excited about the prospect of future *Vampire Academy* films."

—Sami Gayle on Mark Waters

Director of photography Tony Pierce-Roberts in his element

IN HIS OWN WORDS: TONY PIERCE-ROBERTS
Director of Photography

"I'm responsible for all artistic and technical requirements to do with the photographing of motion pictures with the emphasis on lighting. In particular, all the night sequences were a big challenge, and in using the new digital technology, we were able to achieve this relatively painlessly. The big point about vampire movies, and this is my second after *Underworld*, is that every shot has to be lit, which of course is more time-consuming than shooting during daylight hours. Also, once you're on a night schedule it is difficult to get off it, so one finds oneself, paradoxically, shooting day material, for example, in the middle of the night! As a consequence, on a film like this with a limited budget and high expectations, one has challenges to get all the equipment needed and the time required to utilize it. In particular, I favor 'balloon' lighting (helium-filled balloons with built-in lamps) for a moonlight effect since, as well as looking realistic, they cover a large area and are quick and easy to move about, giving the director maximum time

flexibility in his shooting. I am pleased to say that Mark Waters, the director, and Deepak Nayar, the producer, were very supportive of this, which I think shows in the final product. I felt my relationship with Mark Waters was very good and mutually respectful—although we had the odd confusion between 'American' English expressions and 'English' ones—but the best thing was his sense of humor, which one really appreciates at 2 a.m. on day forty-three of night work. I think what inspired me most on this film was the attitude of the cast, who were, without exception, delightful to work with and very 'gung ho' in their attitude to the material. Given that this film is supposed to take place in a secret Russian academy in the middle of Montana, but in fact was largely shot in a Victorian neo-Gothic school in Surrey and other locations near London—I can't wait to see if we have succeeded in convincing the audience."

"I'm so excited for people to see how awesome the cinematography, costume design, and production design are. Tony Pierce-Roberts, the DP, did such a phenomenal job shooting the movie with a dark underlying tone that helped perpetuate the suspense of the story."
— ZOEY DEUTCH ON TONY PIERCE-ROBERTS

Queen Tatiana parades Lissa Dragomir before the students of St. Vladimir's.

Q&A WITH PRODUCTION DESIGNER
FRANK WALSH

Q: Can you give us a brief description of what your role entails?

My role is to create the whole visual style of the film, from reading the script and analyzing both the books and the culture of the subject, to creating suitable settings for all the scenes. These ranged from built sets on stages to adapted locations or virtual sets created in visual effects.

Q: How did you end up working on *Vampire Academy*?

I was sent a script to read, and then interviewed by Mark Waters. We discussed my ideas, and I submitted a concept sketch that I felt distilled my view of the world we were setting out to capture. Fortunately, it reflected his vision, and I was hired.

Q: Take us through the process of a production designer's initial start. What does that involve?

I start by reading the script and discussing the style of the film with the director. Luckily, Mark was very knowledgeable about all the Vampire Academy books, and gave me insight into the many subplots and backstories, which stretched way beyond the words in the script. It was he who made me aware of Dimitri's interest in the Wild West, which allowed us to create dressing for his room. I then researched the books with an assistant, who helped pull out more details essential to creating a believable world of the Academy. As the available time before filming began was very short, I worked with a group of concept artists, who helped me to quickly draw my ideas, so we could bring the world alive and explain to everyone what they should expect to see on-screen. We also developed all the myriad elements of props and graphics called for in the script; my role is to conceive every

aspect of the film visually and work with the director of photography and visual effects, and steer the production to a cohesive and encompassing design solution.

Q: What is your relationship like with Mark Waters? Was there anything that you both agreed was essential in bringing this story to the screen as cleanly as possible? Was there anything you disagreed about?

The relationship has to be one of close communication and collaboration, although finally it is the director's vision we are making real. We would discuss everything, and I would put forward ideas, which we developed between us. However, we did have some conflicting thoughts—the security center and cells being the most notable, which took a little time in finding a mutually satisfying solution to a problem. The set description in the script merely referred to a "high-tech security center built over old Gothic cells." This statement embodied for me the whole ethos of the design approach, a mix of old and

Production designer Frank Walsh's creative touch is felt on all of the *Vampire Academy* sets.

new. As this was going to have to be a very large set for the action, it was important it had the correct visual impact. My response was to mix hard concrete and modern steel structures within a high-vaulted catacomb made from ancient stones. Originally, I conceived it as many levels of bricked-up niches, coming down to a ground floor where the niches had been converted into prison cells, with automatic sliding glass doors. Access was via a lift passing down behind frosted glass windows in the stacked arches at one end of the space, descending from a dizzying height. Lighting, for me, is a critical part of the visual design, so I conceived this as a dark place, lit from harsh, modern, hanging tubular lights giving a cold quality of light, while the cells had warm daylight entering from air shafts. As the lift descends, it cast shafts of light into the darkened chambers, arriving at the black polished steel security platform level where all the high-tech screens are situated. My concept was to try to create a sense that this massive cathedral space was far below the main school buildings and echoed the cave in which we later see the Strigoi hiding during the day. The director, however, was very keen to create a sense of the vaulted ceiling, so there was a compromise on the height of the

design; but even so, I feel it was a great space and captured the essence of what I wanted. It also defined the colors I used in the film, contrasting a polished gray concrete floor and black polished metal construction, offset by the warm golden tones of the cells and dark gray stone walls.

Q: Were there any surprises you encountered during shooting?

The weather! Given we were shooting in England, one expects wet weather, but we enjoyed quite the reverse. So much so, the grass grew parched and yellow. Referring back again to the color palette I employed, it meant the school not only had a lovely honey-golden stone construction, but it was surrounded by golden fields of grass. In the evening with the falling light and dark sky, it was a truly fantastic setting. Placing the training assault course against this, with its polished silver metalwork, brought the color scheme through again.

Q: What were your conversations like with Richelle Mead? Was she able to illuminate aspects from the books so that it was a seamless transition?

To my great sadness, due to time constraints and access issues, I never had

an opportunity to meet or discuss the subject with Richelle. However, the manner in which she wrote was very graphic, and the director was a great route to the type of detail in the books that I needed to work with. However, I hope on a future occasion there will be an opportunity for closer direct dialogue, as it will only enhance the development of my ideas, allowing me a deeper insight into the less obvious nuances of her stories, drawing on the subtleties that have made these works such a cult hit with their devoted readership, and bringing these to the big screen.

> "And Frank Walsh, the production designer, is a total genius. I was so blown away by the sets he built and the never-ending work he put into this film that I was literally too afraid to say hi to him until Mark forced me to."
> — ZOEY DEUTCH
> ON FRANK WALSH

Q: What excited you most about this project? Is there anything you can't wait for audiences to see?

So many things were exciting to do. The training spaces were fun to design, and in a later book we see Rose graduate by tackling a massive version of this assault course. I always pictured the guardians as modern rock stars, "parkouring" athletes. So their training apparatus had to reflect that. The gyroscopes, for instance, were the first idea—placing them at the extremes of aircrew/astronaut training methods. Then put everything into a rock-and-roll stage environment. I hope this will develop and grow into an amazing structure in future films. It was a fantastic experience, having the subject and the characters' brilliant tools to work with. To have such great female characters to create stages for was unusual, and it was wonderful how the actors responded in such a positive way to the world I created for them. Because in the end, that is a primary role for me, creating environments that both support and enhance the actors' performances. And then, naturally, to define and explain things to an audience that extend beyond that performance.

Dominic Sherwood and Lucy Fry get some direction from Mark Waters.

IN HIS OWN WORDS: CHRIS GILL, *Editor*

"As the editor, I come on board at the start of filming and remain until the end to oversee the entire creative picture and sound processes. For me, once I know I'm cutting the movie, I often immerse myself with relevant music and can easily spend days on research. Having read the script twice, I then try to react to the dailies as a spontaneous process, constantly trying to gauge the tone of the film. My CV is varied, and I actively pursue all genres. It makes me a better editor. I am self-taught and try to watch as many movies as I can . . . not seen many lately, as the schedule for *Vampire Academy* has been relentless! I love the editing process; it's the creative hub of the movie. I'd never worked with Mark before and have found the whole process of collaboration both exciting and stimulating. Quite simply, the cutting room is where the movie lives or dies. The chemistry between the editor and director is key to the movie's success. The big thing was Mark's infectious enthusiasm for the project and the brilliant performance of Zoey Deutch as Rose Hathaway. No favorite moment in the script, but the writing is funny and dynamic. Mark is a dedicated director. His time management skills are superlative. He was aware, at all times, of potential issues developing, and then dealt with them with speed and good humor. And I think we have witnessed the development of a star in the making with Zoey, and her gutsy, honest, witty, and dynamic performance will win over countless fans."

"I'm always worried about how fans of the book will react, but we have kept true to a lot of the books. Obviously there are changes, but with the books as a basis, hopefully the fans will like what we have done."

—DOMINIC SHERWOOD

Vampire Academy's rabid fandom can be felt at the Official *Vampire Academy* Movie Facebook page and @OfficialVAMovie on Twitter.

"The social media following has been phenomenal!" said Sami Gayle. "We are so fortunate to have such a lovely group of *Vampire Academy* fans whose support and encouragement have been wonderful. I hope they enjoy what we've created as much as we enjoyed putting it together. We had a blast!"

Sarah Hyland added, "The *Vampire Academy* fans have been so amazing to us from the very beginning. Of course I'm worried how they will react. I want them to be over the moon about the whole project because it's so important. We wouldn't be anywhere without the fans, so I hope with every fiber of my being that they love it just as much, if not more than the books."

RICHELLE MEAD ON THE
Fan Reaction to the Movie

"I see a lot of long-term fans, people who are following me into the Bloodlines series, who are going back and rereading the Vampire Academy books so they can be up to speed on it. They are super enthusiastic, and I think it's really amazing that the people working on the movie and the cast are so active online, as well. They feel very accessible, and I think that a lot of the fans feel connected, and not just to be as they have in the past, but also to these people, 'cause they are open—as much as they can be, of course—about what they are doing and how excited they are for the project. They have just generated a lot of enthusiasm for it that is spreading to readers, as well."[18]

The official *Vampire Academy* Facebook and Twitter pages have been crucial in not only galvanizing the fans but also directly involving them in the filmmaking process. Not content with posting simple updates, the team behind these pages created the hash tag #BestFandomEver so that fans could share their thoughts and engage the producers directly through lengthy Q&A sessions. It was here where rumors were quickly squashed, creative choices were justified, and anticipated casting announcements were made. Fans were taken behind the scenes in a way they hadn't experienced before, proving that the #VAFamily weren't simply a tool to be used—they were a welcome part of the journey.

ON PLEASING *the Fans*

"Of course it's a little nerve-racking, because you want to serve the books and character the right way. But once you're on set, you're really just thinking about doing your job the best you can."—**Zoey Deutch**

"I'm always worried about how fans of the book will react, but we have kept true to a lot of the books. Obviously there are changes, but with the books as a basis, hopefully the fans will like what we have done."—**Dominic Sherwood**

"I love the books, so I really wanted to keep Lissa as true to the book as possible, though in the film script she came across a little bolder. I know what it is like to have a magical world in your mind, and then Hollywood turns it into a movie and you can never get your personal images back again. It's really hard to let go and embrace the new interpretation because it's never the way you imagined it. But I really think fans will love the film for having a life of its own. When I asked Richelle about what the biggest difference was between the world she created in her book and what she saw on set, she said that everything was much grander. Hopefully fans will like this version, and find a way to hold onto their imaginary worlds, too."—**Lucy Fry**

RICHELLE MEAD ON THE
Books' Popularity

"Vampire Academy's success was a gradual, steady climb. There are a lot of young-adult books these days that are sold in big, flashy deals, with tons of promo that put them on top of the best-seller charts with the first book. That wasn't the case with *Vampire Academy*, which had a much quieter start. Nonetheless, word of mouth spread quickly, and even by the second book, I'd seen a notable jump in both sales and e-mail I was getting from readers hooked on the books. A similar spike happened with *Shadow Kiss*, and by the time the next book, *Blood Promise*, came out, the series had such a big following that bookstores weren't prepared for the turnout I was getting at signings. That gradual growth really helped ease me into this world and has made me extremely grateful for the success the series has earned. It's a testament to the story as well, and readers' love for it, that the series was able to gather that kind of momentum and following on its own without such early buzz. It means a lot to me that fans are as attached to the characters as I am."

#VAFamily

"The #VAFamily are all one unit. We are so supportive of each other and we really do feel like a family. Being on Twitter for a few years and watching the fan base grow, we welcome the newcomers and never have we had an argument. Also, we do feel very fortunate with the amount of attention we get from Richelle Mead and @OfficialVAMovie. Almost every day, @OfficialVAMovie is responding and retweeting fans. We are also very supportive of the cast members and their activities and work beyond the film. I have great faith and trust in Richelle Mead as the creator of the story; if she was happy, then so was I. When I found out about the team behind the production, all my concerns were gone. With Mark Waters as the director and Daniel Waters handling the screenplay, I knew *Vampire Academy* was in great hands. Even more so, the casting by Marci Liroff was perfect." —**Sydney Rose, @VampAcademyAus**

"My love for *Vampire Academy* and the fandom is why I started Her Royal Guardian. I wanted to have a place to pour my obsession into and document the journey of the book and movie. As a longtime fan of *Vampire Academy*, I also wanted to be able to connect with fans on another level, by not only updating fans on the latest news and articles about the books and movie, but by also discussing the series and world and interacting through our discussion features and questions. *Vampire Academy* is so different from many of the YA series that are popular at the moment. Rose is this strong, badass character that's already in this supernatural world, rather than a character who innocently stumbles across it. For me, *Vampire Academy* is a book about being a young adult and growing up and finding who you are."
—Paige Barker, owner of Her Royal Guardian (herroyalguardian.com)

"We refer to our fandom as the #VAFamily because we interact like family. We get along and have so many similar interests. We've yet to experience any negatives, and everyone is supportive of each other. It's the best fandom to be a part of. The fun part about Twitter and having a *Vampire Academy* fan page is that we've chatted with Richelle, as well as many cast members, and that's exciting! Some of the cast even follow us back, and it just goes to show how awesome the #VAFamily truly is. We are truly a happy and supportive group of worldwide fans!"—Maria L. Garcia, @VAfandomUSA

"Of course it's a little nerve-racking, because you want to serve the books and character the right way. But once you're on set, you're really just thinking about doing your job the best you can."

—ZOEY DEUTCH

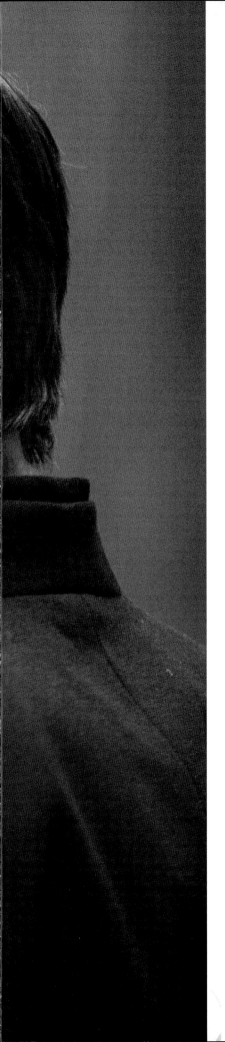

"Richelle did a wonderful job of capturing teenage emotion and letting girls or boys find something to relate to by letting us know that we are not alone. I wanted to connect with people who share the love that I have for this book. This has been one of the best experiences of my life. I am so thankful that I am a part of a family like this. We support each other, from promoting trends that are going to take place to passing around edits that other people have done. Richelle is such a sweetheart and takes time out of her busy life to answer questions that the fans may have about the movie or any about her upcoming projects.

"One time during a Q&A, I asked her how her son was doing. She responded, telling me that he was well and saying she was thankful for my question. One thing that has surprised me is how close we are. If someone in this fan base has a bad day and needs to talk, someone is there to listen. I have made so many friends from around the world. I would have never met these people if it were not for *Vampire Academy*." —**Ashten Healy, @va_rosemarie**

RICHELLE MEAD ON
Fan Interaction

"Signings are my favorite part of the book promo process. So much of the job of writing books is spent cooped up in my office, and it's so, so powerful for me to get out there and meet the people who are actually affected by the work I do alone all day. I'm not sure I could pick one favorite story when there are just so many wonderful ones I've heard from fans. I've had people tell me how the books got them through difficult times, like a divorce or military tour of duty. I've had people tell me how they didn't like to read until they found my books. I've seen the books bring people together, like mothers and daughters who *finally* have a shared interest, or friends who met at school through the books. All of those stories are little gems for me, and I treasure all of them. They help motivate me when I go back home and begin the long hours of writing a new book. Those stories make me want to keep delivering the best books I can."

Once again I must thank the producers, cast, and crew of *Vampire Academy* for lending me their time and shedding some light on the mythical process of filmmaking. We are all the wiser for it.

— *Brandon T. Snider*

Rob Valois—Thank you for giving me an opportunity to play in a new sandbox. As a writer, I enjoyed the challenge. It kept me on my toes. As a person, I still don't know why you required me to give a blood sacrifice, but whatever. Your calm, cool demeanor helped me from descending into insanity, and I appreciate your encouragement. But next time let's give ourselves some more time, okay?

Richelle Mead—Without you none of this would be possible. I mean, we know that already (in a space-time continuum kind of way), but you were always our ace in the hole, and we couldn't be happier to have received your blessing. Thank you so much and congratulations on all your success.

Daniel Waters and Marci Liroff—You went above and beyond the call of duty, and I'm grateful for your contributions. This book is all the better because of your wisdom.

Brandy Colbert and Sara Kreger—Copyediting this manuscript isn't one of those things you do with a glass of wine on a veranda one afternoon. Or maybe it is and you're that good. Either way, thank you and I would appreciate it if you kept all of my grammatical secrets (there's money in it for you).

Neo9 Design, Inc. (neo9design.com)—My original concept for the design of this book was to just draw happy faces everywhere . . . thank you for talking me out of that. Your hard work shows and you make the words look good. I can't ask for more than that.

The Fans—A very special "thank you" goes out to Laura Lock, Bailey Riddle, Michella Domenici, Ashten Healy, Maria L. Garcia, and Paige Barker. We appreciate every ounce of support from the #VAFamily, and I hope you all enjoy the book.

Erin Stein—Who knew after all these years (three?) that a simple conversation about buttons would ultimately bring me to this experience. You rock. Thanks for the good word.

Jim McCarthy—Thank you for working your magic!

Travis Kramer, Paul Marlow, John Domingos, and Caitlin Hunt—Each of you helped make this book possible in some form or another, and you each get one piece of candy next time I see you.

Terry and Jean Snider—Without your support I'd probably be living under a bridge eating cat food and talking to a stuffed animal for most of the day. I'm forever grateful for your love and encouragement, despite my deep desire to actually dig into some tuna and roll around in the sewer.

Brandon T. Snider has authored the award-winning *The Dark Knight Manual* as seen in *Entertainment Weekly*, *Time*, and *Wired*. He's penned over twenty-five books featuring pop culture's most famous brands such as Superman, Spider-Man, the Muppets, and *Adventure Time*. Brandon has also written for and appeared on Comedy Central's *Inside Amy Schumer*. He applied to the Vampire Academy in order to research this book but was denied because he was "too pale and bloodthirsty," which is kind of rude, right? Brandon lives in New York City where he's a member of SAG-AFTRA and the Writers Guild of America. On the Internet you can find him at cootiekid.com, but, please, be gentle.

Notes

1. Michelle Rowen, *Vampire Academy: The Ultimate Guide* (New York: Razorbill, 2011).
2. Sabrina Rojas Weiss, "'Vampire Academy' Author Richelle Mead Excited for Big-Screen Battle," *Hollywood Crush* (blog), MTV.com, December 8, 2010, http://hollywoodcrush.mtv.com/2010/12/08/vampire-academy-movie/.
3. Sabrina Rojas Weiss, "'Vampire Academy' Author Richelle Mead Excited for Big-Screen Battle," *Hollywood Crush* (blog), MTV.com, December 8, 2010, http://hollywoodcrush.mtv.com/2010/12/08/vampire-academy-movie/.
4. Amanda Bell, "Richelle Mead chats up 'Vampire Academy: Blood Sisters,'" Examiner.com, June 19, 2013, http://www.examiner.com/article/exclusive-richelle-mead-chats-up-vampire-academy-blood-sisters/.
5. Jacqueline Andriakos, "'Vampire Academy' motion poster: What does it mean?" *Inside Movies* (blog), *Entertainment Weekly*, July 24, 2013, http://insidemovies.ew.com/2013/07/24/vampire-academy-movie-motion-poster/.
6. Breanne L. Heldman, "Exclusive 'Vampire Academy' Motion Poster Will Stake You For Sure," *Yahoo! Movies* (blog), July 22, 2013, http://movies.yahoo.com/blogs/movie-talk/exclusive-vampire-academy-motion-poster-stake-sure-213347380.html/.
7. Amanda Bell, "Richelle Mead chats up 'Vampire Academy: Blood Sisters,'" Examiner.com, June 19, 2013, http://www.examiner.com/article/exclusive-richelle-mead-chats-up-vampire-academy-blood-sisters/.
8. Amanda Bell, "Richelle Mead chats up 'Vampire Academy: Blood Sisters,'" Examiner.com, June 19, 2013, http://www.examiner.com/article/exclusive-richelle-mead-chats-up-vampire-academy-blood-sisters/.
9. Michelle Rowen, *Vampire Academy: The Ultimate Guide* (New York: Razorbill, 2011).
10. Michelle Rowen, *Vampire Academy: The Ultimate Guide* (New York: Razorbill, 2011).
11. Michelle Rowen, *Vampire Academy: The Ultimate Guide* (New York: Razorbill, 2011).
12. "'Vampire Academy' Author Was 'Astonished' When She Read the Script," *Hollywood Crush* (blog), MTV.com June 20, 2013, http://hollywoodcrush.mtv.com/2013/06/20/vampire-academy-richelle-mead-interview/.
13. Amanda Bell, "Richelle Mead chats up 'Vampire Academy: Blood Sisters,'" Examiner.com, June 19, 2013, http://www.examiner.com/article/exclusive-richelle-mead-chats-up-vampire-academy-blood-sisters/.
14. Amanda Bell, "Richelle Mead chats up 'Vampire Academy: Blood Sisters,'" Examiner.com, June 19, 2013, http://www.examiner.com/article/exclusive-richelle-mead-chats-up-vampire-academy-blood-sisters/.
15. Amanda Bell, "Richelle Mead chats up 'Vampire Academy: Blood Sisters,'" Examiner.com, June 19, 2013, http://www.examiner.com/article/exclusive-richelle-mead-chats-up-vampire-academy-blood-sisters/.
16. Michelle Rowen, *Vampire Academy: The Ultimate Guide* (New York: Razorbill, 2011).
17. Amanda Taylor, "Why 'Vampire Academy' is not 'Twilight': Director Mark Waters Explains," August 23, 2013, http://insidemovies.ew.com/2013/08/23/vampire-academy-director-interview/.
18. Amanda Bell, "Richelle Mead chats up 'Vampire Academy: Blood Sisters,'" Examiner.com, June 19, 2013, http://www.examiner.com/article/exclusive-richelle-mead-chats-up-vampire-academy-blood-sisters/.

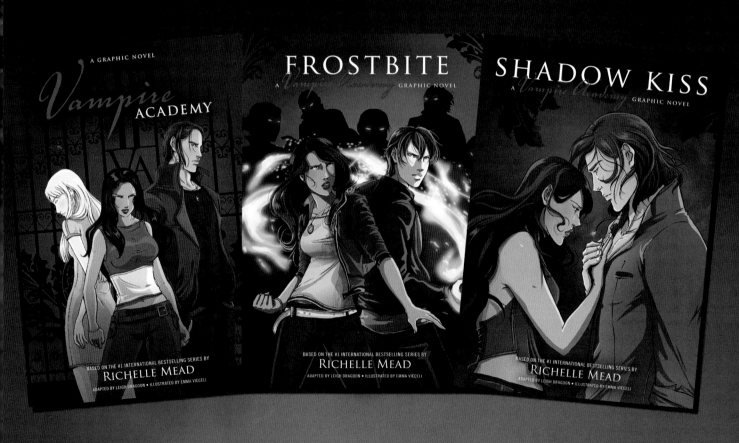

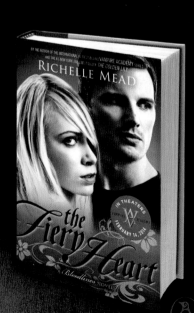

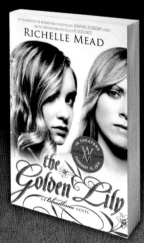

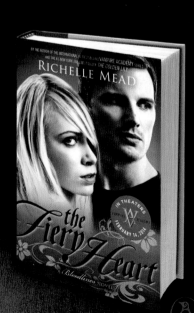